This book was printed in Hong Kong.

Layout Designer: P. Derano

To order additional copies of this book, contact:
Creating A Deer Proof Garden, Ltd
www.creatingadeerproofgarden.com
info@creatingadeerproofgarden.com

Creating A
Deer-Proof Garden

By Peter Derano

Creating a Deer-Proof Garden

**A Complete Description of Deer-Proof Annuals, Perennials,
Ground Covers, Vines, Shrubs, and Trees**

This book will be the last reference you will ever need to create and maintain a worry-free deer-proof garden. As an amateur gardener and landscaper for over thirty years, I have researched and cultivated plants that deer will not eat even in the dead of winter when they are most apt to browse in your garden.

Featuring ***over 117 deer-proof plants with more than 255 full-color photographs,*** you will be able to see deer-proof plants in their full year-round beauty!

Much more than a simple list of plants, my book will give you a full description of each species: the ultimate height and spread, the month the flowers will bloom, the exposure needs (sun, shade, etc.) the type of soil needed to thrive, and the watering and fertilizing needs of each plant.

I also suggest the best use for each plant in terms of where to position them for the best impact and the best results.

This book covers annuals, biennials, perennials, deciduous shrubs and trees, evergreen shrubs and trees, groundcovers, vines and more!

Finally, I advise you which plants should **never** be used in the deer-proof garden and should be avoided at all cost.

Contents

Born out of the frustration of spending thousands of dollars on plantings year after year only to have them destroyed within the same season by a burgeoning population of deer, I have—through trial, error, and experience—come up with a list of deer-proof plants. This will end your frustrations of losing plants to deer. It will also save you a considerable amount of time *and* money in purchasing plants that are not going to be devoured by deer.

Let me say, I find it truly amazing when I walk into a nursery located in areas infested by deer and see rows of azaleas, rhododendrons, and euonymus for sale.

It makes me wonder if anyone is advising the average homeowner which plants are often eaten by deer and which plants are not. After speaking to many salespeople at different nurseries, I find a distinct lack of knowledge about which plants to avoid. There does not seem to be a criteria to work with. The homeowner is often sold plants that are eaten by deer, by nursery salespeople, who should know better. This is not to say that all nurseries are irresponsible in their sale of plants. I know of many nurseries that will guide the customer to the correct species for their situation; however, there seems to be a don't-ask-don't-tell attitude out there concerning plants often devoured by deer.

This is the reason for my book. If I can save the average homeowner the time, money, effort and frustration, I have put in my home garden to create a deer safe garden, then my efforts will be rewarded.

The Problem
White-tailed deer
(*Odocoileus virginianus*)

Let's start by identifying the problem. In the last twenty years, the deer population in the United States has grown dramatically. Presently, there are over thirty million white-tailed deer in North America! There are a number of reasons for the staggering increase in the deer population. First and foremost, their natural habitat has been greatly reduced by urban sprawl. There simply is less open space for them to graze. The growing demand for a country lifestyle by humans has gradually destroyed deer's natural habitat. In losing their natural habitat, instead of slowing their growth number as one would think, it has actually increased it. Deer have completely adjusted to surviving in the urban landscape and have grown in number at an alarmingly fast rate.

Their natural predators such as the wolf and coyotes are practically nonexistent in most high-population regions while at the same time, the deer population is growing in these same regions. Finally, the milder winters we have experienced in the last twenty years has reduced the amount of snow cover, which allows deer to graze on plants and thus survive the winter.

All in all, the above suggests a cycle that will not change anytime soon. Local governments will not condone the culling of the deer population (nor do I personally). Relocation is a huge expense and not realistic. Birth control methods are yet unproven and expensive, and the long-term effects are unknown.

The only plausible solution is to live with the deer.

Looking at the problem on this basis, I find the best solution is to design gardens that will not ring the dinner bell for deer. I feel it is far better and much cheaper to purchase hay to feed the deer during the lean months of winter than to grow plants that they are attracted to if you are inclined to feed deer.

Feeding Habits of Deer

Most homeowners' plantings are consumed by deer from the beginning of the first frost through early spring. This is a time when our landscape plants are most vulnerable. Deer primarily feed in the woods on understory plants in their native habitat, which are woodlands. Generally, deer will only browse woody plants (tress, shrubs, and certain vines) during the winter months between November through April. The occasional exceptions in areas with severe deer problems seems to be yews (Taxus varieties) and evergreen Euonymus varieties, which will be eaten during the warmer seasons. Different parts of plants are eaten by deer at different times during the year. In the fall and winter, they browse and eat woody material as not much else is available at that time. In the spring, they revert to browsing foliage.

Deer do not feel comfortable feeding around our homes and would prefer to stay in the relative safety and cover of the woods. They are extremely adaptable; for this reason, most deer will forage at dusk to dawn, where there is less chance of human contact. During the spring and summer time, the majority of the herd will stay in their natural habitat and away from our plantings. Of course, some plant species are irresistible to deer, and they will browse these plants on our property during the spring and summer. I must tell you, certain plant species are like candy to deer and should be avoided at all cost. (Later on in this book, I will list these plants.)

Deer will go to extremes to browse on plants they like. For example, most deer will stand on their hind legs to browse on tasty shrubs or higher branches of trees. In doing so, they can reach a height of 4 ½–6 feet! They will breeze past plants giving off a distasteful aroma to get to a plant they prefer.

Deer-Proof Alternatives

Deer-Repellent Spray
Deer-repellent sprays do work for a short period of time; my experience is about five to seven weeks. Most makers advise their products will last up to eight weeks. The key words here being "up to," really means the product works for eight weeks in your garden, but in your neighbor's garden across town, it could only work for five weeks. It really depends on the size of the deer population grazing in your exact environment, the time of the year, and other factors. If you use these sprays, understand that the window for good performance is between five to eight weeks; after the fifth week, start to closely monitor your plants for damage.

Deer-repellent sprays perform either through a scent or taste deterrent or a combination of the two. In other words, the smell or the taste of the spray will repel deer after they come in contact with it. The scent activated sprays must be reapplied after each rainfall. The taste-activated sprays gradually start to lose their effectiveness after the spray becomes dissipated throughout the plant, which generally takes a few weeks.

According to the makers of these products, deer will remember the scent or taste associated with these sprays and will not browse these plants again. I do not agree with this; there are just too many deer actively feeding in our home areas. If in fact deer do have a memory of this, it is certain that their relatives will try a few bites of a favorite plant species even if recently sprayed.

In addition, new shoots (new growth) will need to be sprayed as these areas were not protected. This entails constant maintenance on many, many plantings in the average home landscape. It is important to note, deer repellents are less effective during the colder winter months than they are during the spring and summer months. This means frequent spraying during the coldest months of the year. In addition, the instructions from the makers are not to spray when the temperature is below thirty-five degrees. What do you do in January when the temperature is fiteen degrees and your five-to-eight-week window is up?

The makers of these products each use a slightly different scent or taste in their ingredients. Some makers use an egg-derived taste and scent while others utilize a mint-based formula. Recently, a pepper taste and scent was developed using red and black pepper mixed with Tabasco. Another recent development is a liquid blood-meal mix. These last two repellents only last about two weeks and must be reapplied after each rainfall. I have tested both the pepper spray and the blood meal and have found the results to be less than satisfactory.

I have found that by changing the product used on each spraying, you are changing the scent or the taste of each plant sprayed. This switching seems to baffle deer for a short while. I have heard many times over the years—from garden centers, landscapers, and professionals in the field—about how a "new" deer repellent is working better than the old standby. The next season, they report the new product is performing like the more established products.

It seems to me that deer may have an acquired-taste mentality. I found over time that when the same spray is applied repeatedly, its effectiveness is greatly reduced. Deer simply become accustomed to the taste or the scent and continue to browse. I have heard of some success with deer sprays from neighbors and others where only one application works even beyond the 8 week window. I feel I should mention this as well. For a quick fix, short-term solution, deer-repellent sprays are a reasonable choice. It is not the long-term answer however.

Nets

I have used nets for the last twenty years. There are several problems associated with their use. There are basically two ways of using nets.

The first is to construct a netted fence using metal or wood stakes for pillars. This is usually the most effective method, but it has some drawbacks. They are generally unsightly to look at. After a short period of time, bucks will use their antlers to tear through the nets or to rip them away from the pillars. Does will use their hoofs to rip through the net or to get underneath it.

Over the winter season, they will create a large-enough opening and in one evening will destroy your plantings. Keep in mind, it takes only one evening to destroy a netted bed of rhododendrons, for example.

The second netting option is placing the nets directly over the plants and pinning the net to the ground using U-shaped pins made of wire. You make the U-shaped pins on your own from heavy-gauge metal wire. This method works to a small degree. The problem is that the deer will eat whatever protrudes through the net. As diligent as you may be in applying the net, when snow falls it will put pressure on the net and force shoots through the openings of the net.

Deer will feed on these shoots as they protrude through the nets, and this will create unsightly plants in spring as most of the flower buds will be missing. Frost will heave the pins from the ground and will enable deer to get under the nets and feed. The end result, at best, is a half-eaten plant that is unsightly to look at and not healthy.

Milorganite

This is a natural fertilizer that works fairly well in keeping deer away for a short time. Its primary use is as a fertilizer, but it is known to keep deer away by its rather nasty scent. It works to some degree because its scent is quite powerful.

The problem is that it must be reapplied every week in order to be effective as deer repellent. I find that it works only on small plantings such as annuals and perennials. It is not effective on shrubs and trees as a deer repellent because the fertilizer is applied to the ground while shrub and tree foliage are too far away from the ground for the scent to be effective in deterring deer from feeding on it. Rain will also decrease its effectiveness rapidly.

The first snow cover will, in effect, neutralize it as a deer repellent.

The obvious problem is that there is a danger in applying too much fertilizer to any plant, especially during its non-growing season.

I do recommend Milorganite during the growing seasons of spring and summer as a natural fertilizer with a secondary side benefit as a deer repellent. It is not nearly the total solution as a deer repellent, but it is effective for a short period.

Human Hair

I have taken human hair cuttings, placed them in a women's nylon stocking, and hung them from shrubs, trees, or whatever. For a very short period (about one week), this may work as the scent of humans frighten deer. It is short-lived as with each rainfall the scent gradually disappears. It is also kind of silly looking.

Soap

I read somewhere a long time ago that by placing scented soap shavings in a women's nylon stocking and positioning them on branches of tree and shrubs will actually repel deer.

I tried this for a whole spring season about fifteen years ago; it certainly promoted many inquisitive questions from visitors.

What are those things hanging from every plant?

Aside from looking ridiculous, after each rain, the soap scent gradually disappeared; and while you do have cleaner plants, it really had no impact on the deer, I am sorry to report.

Predator Urine

If you can find it at a local nursery or through a mail-order house, this will be effective for a short period of time. It will keep the deer away while its scent lasts. There may be some nibbling after it is first sprayed on the plants, but after the first taste, they will not come back until the scent dissipates. Depending on the rainfall, it will need to be applied every ten to fifteen days. I do not consider this the ultimate solution; it is expensive, high maintenance, and not long lasting. Anyway, who wants to be out there in the dead of winter spraying coyote urine on a large-scale garden?

As you can see, I have tried every method known to keep my plantings protected from deer without success or with very little success.

It finally occurred to me to use plantings that deer do not eat.

This is the final and best solution.

While it is true that some of the most popular plant species such as rhododendrons, azaleas, euonymus, impatiens, etc., are not to be used in a deer-proof garden, I can guarantee you color throughout the growing season and, along with that, the peace of mind that comes with understanding that your plants will survive the winter months and not be eaten down to the ground by deer.

Finally, before going further, I want you to note, although my *Deer-Proof Gardening* book will offer you a garden that deer will not feed upon, it is important that you understand that the plants' success totally hinges upon your ability as a gardener!

Consider what I mean.

When you start with the planting, be guided with the following questions:
1. Is the selected plant listed in the correct landscape climate zone for your home area?
2. Is the plant going to be positioned in the best location for it in terms of exposure to sun, shade, etc.?
3. Is the soil to the plant's preference?
4. Did you dig the proper hole size for the plant?
5. Did you add any amenities to the soil?
6. Did you plant it at the proper planting height?

After planting, be guided with the following questions.
1. Are you watering appropriately?
2. Insect control - Are you checking every two weeks or so for signs of feeding or nesting?
3. Disease control - Are you checking every two weeks for signs of disease (powdery mildew, etc.)?
4. Are you fertilizing each fall and the following spring?

I point out these tasks to illustrate a lot more goes into maintaining the deer-proof garden than just planting a shrub that deer will not find tasty and forgetting about it.

Think how beautiful your garden really can be. It takes a little effort, but the joy of getting up in the morning and knowing that your newly planted shrubs were not eaten overnight by hungry deer makes it all worth it!

A final word about deer-proof plants:

Many of the experts in the field will argue that there are very few deer-proof plants.
To a degree, that may be correct. It depends, frankly, on your definition of "deer-proof plants." To me, a plant that *may* be occasionally lightly browsed by deer constitutes a deer-proof plant. A plant that is missing a few leaves because of occasional browsing is still a fully functional plant.
It will continue to grow, to flower, and to thrive in spite of the infrequent browsing that may occur.
This is my definition of a deer-proof plant: a plant that *may* occasionally be very lightly browsed, yet it still maintains its shape and continues to grow well.

Having said this, it is entirely possible that all the plants described in this book will be totally deer proof in your garden. It really depends on your exact environment, the size of the deer population in your area, and the time of the year. What I can tell you is none of the plants described in my guide will be eaten down to the ground and need to be replaced because of deer browsing.

Climate Zones

A climate-zone map divides the country into several climate zones, linking areas with similar climates together. This zone map is a tool for gardeners to discover where their home climate zone falls and, more importantly, which plant species will survive in their home zone. For a shrub, perennial, or tree to survive and grow year after year, the plant must tolerate year-round conditions in your home area, such as the lowest and highest temperatures. The temperature mentioned in each zone represents the *coldest* temperature that will fall in each area.

Generally speaking, this guide is created for gardens in landscape climate zones 4 through 9. These zones have a temperature range of -30 degrees (below zero) to 30 degrees (above zero). Although this covers a huge range of temperatures, it is important you know where your home garden falls in the landscape map below. By checking the climate zone of each plant you are interested in, you will find deer-proof plants that will work in zones *other* than zones 4 to 9. You should determine your own zone and choose only the plants suitable for your area. Understand which trees, shrubs, and flowers work best in your climate. A good idea is to check with your local nursery to see which deer-proof plant species are available. If your local garden center is stocking a species, it is a good bet that it is hardy in your home area.

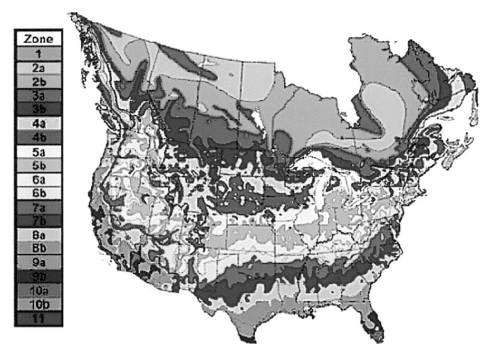

Average Annual Minimum Temperature					
Zone	Temperature °C	Temperature °F	Zone	Temperature °C	Temperature °F
1	-45.6 and below	below -50	6b	-17.8 to -20.5	0 to -5
2a	-42.8 to 45.5	-45 to -50	7a	-15.0 to -17.7	5 to 0
2b	-40.0 to -42.7	-40 to -45	7b	-12.3 to -15.0	10 to 5
3a	-37.3 to -40.0	-35 to -40	8a	-9.5 to -12.2	15 to 10
3b	-34.5 to -37.2	-30 to -35	8b	-6.7 to -4.0	20 to 15
4a	-31.7 to -34.4	-25 to -30	9a	-3.9 to -6.6	25 to 20
4b	-28.9 to -31.6	-20 to -25	9b	-1.2 to -3.8	30 to 25
5a	-26.2 to -28.8	-15 to -20	10a	1.6 to -1.1	35 to 30
5b	-23.4 to -26.1	-10 to -15	10b	4.4 to 1.7	40 to 35
6a	-20.6 to -23.3	-5 to -10	11	4.5 and above	40 and above

Deer-Proof Perennials

Perennials are plants whose foliage and flowers disappear or die back during winter. The root system stays alive during this time, and the plant goes into a sort of hibernation if you will. After this resting period, during the spring, new growth will appear, announcing the coming of a new gardening period.

Perennials have been cultivated and used for thousands of years; many varieties are ancient in age and are still widely used today. The advantages of growing perennials are many. In early spring, the average gardener will have a base of plants in their border each year to build around with annuals or other plants as the growing season begins. They often save time, labor, and money in replanting each spring. The wide array of flower choices and the texture of the foliage of perennials are unsurpassed in the landscape world. Perennials do require some loving care though. Soil must be amended each spring; heavy feeding is needed to give the plants a jump start. Insects and disease can plague certain species. I consider this group of plants more high maintenance than most, but it is worth the effort.

Fortunately, many varieties of perennials are deer proof, providing you with great color and texture the entire growing season!

Achillea (filipendulina and *milefolium)*
Fernleaf Yarrow

Description – Yarrow is a very unusual plant with both attractive and interesting flowers and foliage. The *filipendulina* and *milefolium* species are the most popular species of this group. Both are very similar in appearance, the notable exception being that *milefolium* has slightly larger flowers. Both species are very suitable for borders and rock gardens. All yarrow foliage is fernlike in appearance with large clusters of tiny flower heads sitting on top of the foliage. Very finely cut, textured leaves give yarrow an exotic look. The foliage is quite dense, almost to the ground and stays striking all season long. Flower color choices range from yellow, to orange, to red with yellow centers—all very attractive. One of the best varieties is fire king, which has a red flower with off-white centers. Golden plate is a yellow-flowering variety with large-size flowers. Yarrow is a medium-size perennial and is best suited in the middle of a border or in a rock garden as a single specimen. Plant yarrow in groups of four to six plants for the best effect, keeping the flower colors all the same.

Zones - 3 to 10

Height - 3 to 4 feet

Spread - 1 to 1.5 feet

Spacing - Plant in groups of three to four, 12 inches apart.

Exposure - full sun, will tolerate light shade

Soil - Yarrow grows best in well-drained, dry soil, but it will tolerate moist soil if not excessively wet.

Bloom time - late June–mid-July

Care - Yarrow is easy to maintain. Water moderately and do not water late in the day. It is subject to stem rot and powdery mildew in moist soils and climates. Yarrow needs to be divided every three to four years for best results; this should be done in early fall or spring.

Achillea milefolium
Fire King

Achillea filipendulina
Golden Plate

Achillea filipendulina
Summer Pastels

Anemone
Japanese Anemone

Description - Anemones are very attractive perennials valued for their late bloom period and showy flowers. The flowers are between 1.5 to 3 inches in size, depending on the variety. Flower colors range from white to pink, to red, to a striking magenta- all with bold, contrasting centers. The foliage stays handsome all season long with it's dark green leaves that are larger at the bottom of the plant and becoming smaller toward the top of the plant. Anemone is very suitable for borders and perennial beds as it stay inbounds, never becoming unruly or invasive. Anemone is a medium-size perennial; position it in the middle of a border. It is also excellent for cut flowers. A few excellent varieties are party dress, which features soft pink flowers with gold centers, and blue shadows, which has blue flowers with yellow centers. Plant anemone in groups of three to four plants for the best effect.

Zones - 6 to 10

Height - 2 to 5 feet

Spread - 1.5 feet

Spacing - 16 to 18 inches apart

Exposure - Partial shade is best, but they will tolerate full sun.

Soil - Anemone grows best in well-drained, moist soil rich in humus. They will not tolerate wet soil in winter as they must have good drainage.

Bloom time - late summer

Care - Anemone is moderately easy to maintain. Water during dry, hot spells in summer. Anemone is subject to black blister beetle, which can quickly defoliate the plant.
It normally does not need to be divided.

Japanese Anemone
Hupehensis japonica
Party Dress

Anemone coronaria spp.

Anemone blanda
Blue Shadows

Aquilegia
Columbine

Description - Columbine is suitable for borders, woodland gardens, and rock gardens. It is highly prized for its ability to lighten up a shady spot with color. The foliage is a light green or silver color that is notched and quite delicate. While the foliage is very attractive, the real stars are the flowers, which are bell shaped and beautiful. Flower sizes vary from 2 inches to 4 inches in size. Color choice can be daunting as columbine is available in a wide variety of colors. White, yellow, pink, magenta, and even a spectacular series of blue colors are available. McKana's giant is an excellent variety, growing 4 feet tall with a wide selection of color choices. Columbine is fully hardy as it is a native plant, growing naturally in our woodlands. It is a small-to-medium-size perennial that works well in the middle of a border. It is also a solid choice as a specimen in the rock garden. Another good use for columbine is in a natural wildflower meadow. It is an excellent choice for its cut flowers as well.

Zones - 3 to 10

Height - 1.5 to 3 feet

Spread - 1 to 2 feet

Spacing - Plant in groups of two to three, 1 to 2 feet apart.

Exposure - Partial shade is best.

Soil - Columbine grows best in well-drained soil rich in humus/organic matter.

Bloom time - late May–mid-June

Care - Columbine can be difficult to maintain. I find them a little on the fussy side. Water regularly and feed it with a light fertilizer regularly (once a week). It is subject to leaf miners, aphids, and columbine borers. Columbine must have a well-drained soil in order to thrive.

Aquilegia x hybrida
McKana's Giant

Aquilegia vulgaris
Winky Blue - White

Aquilegia x hybrida
Mckana' Giant

Artemisia schmidtiana
Silver Mound, Wormwood

Description –Silver mound has wonderful silvery gray, green foliage that is featherlike in appearance. Although it does flower, the flowers are hardly noticeable; the star is the foliage rather than the flowers, which are small and inconspicuous. The foliage is dense, grows in a mound shape, and stays striking all season long. It is very widely used in borders and rock gardens toward the front as a low grower. Silver mound is half to fully hardy. Plant it in groups of three to four plants for the best effect.

Zones - 4 to 9

Height - 1 to 1.5 feet

Spread - 1 to 1.5 feet

Spacing - Plant in groups of three to four, 20 to 24 inches apart

Exposure - full sun

Soil - Silver mound grows best in well-drained, dry soil that is not too rich in organic matter. It will not tolerate moist soil.

Bloom time - The foliage stays attractive all season long.

Care - Silver mound is easy to maintain. Water moderately and do not water late in the day.
It is subject to rust, but this can be remedied by spraying. It rarely, if ever, needs to be divided.

Artemisia schmidtiana
Silver Mound

Aruncus dioicus
Goatsbeard

Description - Due to its large size, goatsbeard works well in the border, positioned toward the rear. It is indeed a large perennial that is more shrublike in appearance than perennial. Goatsbeard is similar in appearance to astilbe but much larger in size. The flowers are very small, but they bloom together creating a featherlike white plume that can be up to 14 inches long. The flowering plume effect is also very similar to astilbe's flowers, but again the plumes are much larger in size than astilbe's. Goatsbeard foliage is an attractive medium green color. Each leaf is medium in size with a fine texture and stays striking all season long. Goatsbeard is not invasive and will not overgrow its boundaries in the border. It also works well in a rock garden as a specimen plant. Plant it in groups of two to three plants for the best effect.

Aruncus dioicus spp.

Zones - 3 to 9

Height - 5 to 6.5 feet

Spread - 3 to 5 feet

Spacing - Plant in groups of two to three, 3 to 5 feet apart

Exposure - partial shade under a high canopy.

Soil - Goatsbeard grows best in well-drained, moist soil that is rich in organic matter.

Bloom time - mid-June–early July

Care - Goatsbeard is easy to maintain. Water moderately and do not water late in the day. It has no serious pests. It rarely, if ever, needs to be divided; dividing is usually not successful.

Asclepias tuberosa
Butterfly Weed

Description - Butterfly weed is a spectacular native plant that will attract butterflies, hummingbirds, and bees to your garden. The flowers are very attractive, and although small, they appear in dense clusters during midsummer. Flower color choices range from yellow to off-white, to a reddish orange color. The most popular flower choice seems to be the orange color group or the yellow group. Butterfly weed foliage is a dark green color and has a slightly hairy effect. It stays striking all season long. Butterfly weed is not invasive. I feel it works best in a rock garden, but some also use it in a border. It also mixes very well with yarrow in an informal bed. An excellent choice for its bold yellow flowers is hello yellow. Plant butterfly weed in groups of two to three plants for the best effect.

Zones - 3 to 9

Height - 1.5 to 2.5 feet

Spread - 1 to 1.5 feet

Spacing - Plant in groups of two to three, 6 to 12 inches apart.

Exposure - full sun

Soil - Butterfly weed grows best in a well-drained, sandy soil. It does not perform well in wet or heavy clay soil.

Bloom time - mid-July–mid-August

Care - Butterfly weed is easy to maintain. Water moderately and do not water late in the day. It has no serious pest problems. It rarely, if ever, needs to be divided as dividing is usually not successful.

Asclepias tuberosa **spp.**

Asclepias tuberosa
Hello Yellow

Aster
Hardy Aster

Description - A member of the daisy family, aster is a hardworking plant that is widely used for good reason. There are hundreds of aster varieties available today with a daunting array of flower choices. The flowers range in color from blue to purple, to pink or white, almost all with yellow centers creating a beautiful contrast. Each flower is about 2 inches in size, very showy, and produced in large clusters. The foliage is of medium texture and dark green in color, staying attractive all season long. Aster is not invasive, never growing out of bounds. It works well in a border, positioned toward the front or the middle. It is effective in a rock garden as well. Aster will attract butterflies as an added benefit. Plant aster in groups of four to five plants for the best effect.

Zones - 4 to 9

Height - 10 inches to 3 feet

Spread - 1 to 1.5 feet

Spacing - Plant in groups of four to five, 12 to 18 inches apart.

Exposure - full sun to partial shade

Soil - Aster grows best in a well-drained, light soil that is not too rich in organic matter.

Bloom time - mid-August—mid-October depending on the variety

Care — Aster can be moderately difficult to maintain. They do not like wet or heavy soils especially in winter, which will promote rotting. Japanese beetles can be a serious pest. Mildew, slugs, and snails can also present a problem. Dividing should be done every two to three years, it is an excellent way to increase stock. Dividing is best done in early spring. Water moderately and do not water late in the day.

Aster frikartii
Flora's Deight

Aster novae angliae
Purple Dome

Aster dumosus
Rose Serenade

Aster novi belgii
Prof. Anton Kippenberg

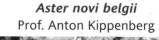

Astilbe
False Spirea

Description - Astilbe is an excellent choice for shady gardens. In fact, astilbe is one of my absolute favorite perennials! It always seems to stay neat and compact in its growth.
A medium-size perennial, astilbe is almost fernlike in appearance. The very attractive flowers are small and together create a featherlike plume that can be up to 16 inches long. Flower colors range from pink to lavender, to white, to red. All astilbe flower colors are quite striking although I find the soft pastel colors standout better and are more widely used than red as example. The foliage is a dark green color with dissected leaves giving a very fine texture to each leaf. The astilbe leaves remind me of

Astilbe × Arendsii cattleya

some species of red maple (acer) with their finely sculpted leaves. Astilbe foliage stays striking all season long. A very popular cultivar is bridal veil, which has beautiful white plumes. Another well-known variety is cattleya, which has vivid pink plumes. Astilbe is not invasive and very restrained in its growth. It works well when positioned both in the middle of a border or in a rock garden. Plant astilbe in groups of three to four plants for the best effect. I recommend using one color per group for the most impact.

Zones - 6 to 10

Height - 1 to 2.5 feet

Spread - 1 to 2.5 feet

Spacing - Plant in groups of three to four, 1 to 2 feet apart.

Exposure - Partial shade to full shade is best, but it will accept full sun if watered heavily.

Soil - Astilbe grows best in a moist soil that is rich in organic matter.

Bloom time - mid-June–early July

Care - Astilbe is fairly easy to maintain. Japanese beetles can be serious pests. Snails and slugs also present problems. Divide every three to four years for best results. Divide in early spring. Water moderately and do not water late in the day.

Astilbe × arendsii
Bridal Veil

Astilbe × Arendsii
Bressingham Beauty

Aurinia saxatilis
Basket of Gold

Description - Basket of gold is favored as a low-growing, spreading perennial. It is a small plant that stays compact in size. The flowers are very small but bloom together, creating a yellow mass that blooms from the top of the plant to the bottom. In bloom, it is very striking as the yellow flower color is quite bright and stands out from a distance. The foliage is small in size with elongated green or gray color leaves and stays attractive all season long. Basket of gold is not invasive as it is a slow grower. It works best in a rock garden or in the front of a border. Plant it in groups of three to four plants for the best effect.

Zones - 4 to 9

Height - 6 to 12 inches

Spread - 12 to 15 inches

Spacing - Plant in groups of three to four, 10 to 12 inches apart.

Exposure - full sun

Soil - Basket of gold grows best in a well-drained, light soil that is not rich in organic matter.

Bloom time - mid-April–mid-May

Care - Basket of gold is fairly easy to maintain. It has no serious pest problems. After blooming, cut the plants in one-half to maintain strong growth. Division is definitely needed every other year. Water moderately and do not water late in the day.

Aurinia saxatilis

Baptisia australis
False Indigo

Description - False indigo is a large perennial that is almost shrub like in appearance. It is an excellent choice for a background plant and should be positioned in the rear of the border. The flowers are about one inch in size and vary in color from light lavender to a dark purple. They appear in long spikes at the end of stout branches. The foliage is a bright green color, and each leaf is medium size. The foliage stays good-looking all season long; at first frost, the foliage becomes black, which creates a very dramatic effect. False indigo is not invasive. Many gardeners consider false indigo the easiest perennial to grow as it has no pests and requires very little attention. Plant it in groups of two to three plants for the best effect.

Zones - 3 to 10

Height - 5 to 6.5 feet

Spread - 3 to 5 feet

Spacing - Plant in groups of two to three, 3 to 5 feet apart.

Exposure - partial shade under a high canopy

Soil - Baptisia grows best in well-drained, moist soil that is rich in organic matter.

Bloom time - mid-June–early July

Care - Baptisia is easy to maintain. It has no serious pest problems. It rarely, if ever, needs to be divided as dividing is usually not successful. Water moderately and do not water late in the day.

***Baptisia australis* spp.**

***Baptisia australis* spp.**

Bergenia cordifolia
Heartleaf Bergenia

Description - Bergenia is a compact plant that is low growing. Its flowers are small but good-looking as they all bloom together. The flowers are about three-fourth inch in size and vary in color from white to light pink. They appear in clusters atop branches about 8 inches above the foliage. Bergenia foliage is medium green and heart shaped; they are striking all season long and in autumn turn from a lush green color to bronze, which creates a dramatic effect. It is one of the least demanding perennials to grow as it has no serious pest problems and requires very little attention. As bergenia is a slow grower, it stays inbounds, never becoming invasive. Bergenia works in a border positioned toward the front or middle as it is a medium-size plant. It is also a very good choice as an edging plant, lining a driveway or walkway. For the best effect, plant bergenia in groups of four to five plants.

Zones - 3 to 9

Height - 12 to 14 inches

Spread - 10 to 16 inches

Spacing - Plant in groups of two to three, 12 to 16 inches apart.

Exposure - tolerates sun or shade

Soil - Bergenia tolerates a wide variety of soils but grows best in a well-drained, average soil.

Bloom time - mid-April–mid-May

Bergenia cordifolia **spp.**

Care - Bergenia is easy to maintain. It has no serious pests. Snails and slugs can be a problem, but are easy to control. They will hide under the dense foliage; you have to pick them by hand. Dividing should be done every three to four years for best results. Water moderately and do not water late in the day.

Bergenia cordifolia **spp.**

Boltonia asteroides
False Chamomile, Pink Beauty

Description - Boltonia is a member of the daisy family. It is an easy-to-grow native plant producing many daisy like flowers on branching stems. The flowers are about three-fourth inch in size and vary in color from white to purple, to blue. Each flower has bright yellow centers creating a great contrast against the flower petals. The foliage is a blue-green color that appears all the way up to the flower head. Boltonia grows in a bushy form and stays attractive all season. It is a large-size perennial, and because of it's height, it works best in the back of a border. It is not invasive and is one of the least-demanding perennials I know of. It has no serious pest problems and requires very little attention. A great variety is pink beauty, which has bright pink flowers with gold centers. For the best effect, plant boltonia in groups of two to three plants, keeping the flower colors the same.

Zones - 3 to 9

Height - 3.5 to 6 feet

Spread - 3 to 3.5 feet

Spacing - Plant in groups of one to two, 4 feet apart.

Exposure - tolerates sun or shade

Soil - Boltonia tolerates a wide variety of soils but grows best in a well-drained soil rich in humus.

Bloom time - mid-August–early October

Care - Boltonia is easy to maintain. It has no serious pests. Dividing should be done every three to four years for best results. Water moderately and do not water late in the day.

Boltonia asteroides
Pink Beauty

Boltonia asteroides

Campanula
Peach-Leaved Bellflower

Description - Bellflower is an easy-to-grow plant with many small single or double flowers on stems about 3 to 4 inches above the foliage. The flowers are about 2 inches in size and are bell shaped. They vary in color from white, to blue, to purple. The blue or purple colors are truly beautiful and the most popular. Foliage is a medium green color and narrow shaped. Bellflower grows in an upright format and stays neat and attractive all season. It is a medium-size perennial and works best in the middle of a border. Bellflower is another non-demanding perennial that has no serious pest problems and requires very little attention. It is not invasive and stays inbounds. An excellent cultivar is blue hybrid.

For the best effect, plant campanula in groups of two to three plants.

Zones - 3 to 10

Height - 1 to 2.5 feet

Spread - 1.5 to 2 feet

Spacing - Plant in groups of two to three, 18 to 22 inches apart.

Exposure - full sun to dappled shade is best

Soil - Campanula tolerates a wide variety of soils but grows best in a moist but well-drained soil rich in humus.

Bloom time - mid-July–end July

Campanula
Blue Hybrid

Campanula
Blue Hybrid

Campanula Medium

Care - Campanula is easy to maintain. It has no serious pests. Dividing should be done every three to four years for best results. It can be prone to crown rot in overly moist conditions. Water moderately and do not water late in the day.

Ceratostigma plumbaginoides
Blue Plumbago

Description – Blue plumbago is
a member of the leadwort
family. It is highly valued
because of its late-season bloom
time. Blue plumbago flowers
when very few perennials are in
bloom. The flowers are about
one-half inch in size, blue upon
opening and gradually change to
violet as the season progresses.
The flowers completely cover
the plant from late August
to the first frost, quite a long
blooming period, and at a time
when only annuals are in bloom.
The foliage stays dense all
season and is dark green color;
in autumn it changes to a deep
red color. Blue plumbago is a
low-growing perennial and works

Ceratostigma plumbaginoides

best in the front of a border or a rock garden or even as an edging plant. It is not demanding to grow either;
it has no serious pest problems and requires very little attention. Blue plumbago is not invasive and will always
stay inbounds. Regular fertilizing and regular watering will promote strong growth. For the best effect, plant it in
groups of four to five plants.

Zones - 5 to 9

Height - 6 to 12 inches

Spread - 14 to 18 inches

Spacing - Plant in groups of four to five, 18 inches apart.

Exposure - tolerates full sun or partial shade

Soil - Blue plumbago tolerates a wide variety of soils but
grows best in a well-drained, rich in humus soil.

Bloom time - late August–early October

Care - Blue plumbago is easy to maintain. It has no
serious pest problems. Dividing is rarely needed. It does
not like excessively wet/soggy soils. Water moderately
and do not water late in the day.

Ceratostigma plumbaginoides

Chrysanthemum coccineum
Painted Daisy

Description - Painted daisy is another member of the daisy family. It is an easy-to-grow plant with many daisy like flowers on branching stems. The flowers are from 2 to 3 inches in size and vary in color from red, pink, or white. Each flower has bright yellow centers. The result is a great contrast and a special flower. The flower colors have a strong painted look to them, which may be a bit garish for some gardeners, but they stand out well from a distance. The foliage is a bright green color and rather sparse with a fine texture. Painted daisy grows in an upright manner and stays attractive all season. It is a medium-size perennial and works best in the middle of a border or a rock garden as a focal point. It is not considered invasive. It has no serious pest problems. For the best effect, plant painted daisy in groups of two to three plants.

Chrysanthemum coccineum

Zones - 5 to 9

Height - 10 inches to 2.5 feet

Spread - 1.5 feet

Spacing - Plant in groups of two to three, 20 inches apart.

Exposure - Full sun is best, but it will tolerate light shade.

Soil - Painted daisy grows best in a well-drained soil, rich in humus.

Bloom time - mid-June—early July

Care - Painted daisy is fairly easy to maintain. It has no serious pest problems. Dividing should be done every four years for best results. Water moderately and do not water late in the day.

Chrysanthemum coccineum
Robinson Hybrids

Chrysanthemum parthenium
Feverfew

Description - Feverfew is a member of the daisy family. It is an easy-to-grow plant with a tremendous amount of daisylike flowers at the end of multi branched stems. The flowers are about three-fourth inch in size and white with bright yellow centers. Although the flowers are small, they are very attractive and bloom together in a great abundance. The foliage is light green in color and small in size although dense. Feverfew grows in a spreading manner and stays low. It should be noted, feverfew can be invasive as the single flowering form will self-sow seed in a generous manner. It is relatively easy to grow except for the removal of unwanted seedlings. Feverfew has no serious pest problems. It is a small-size perennial and works best in the front to middle of a border. For the best effect, plant feverfew in groups of two to three plants.

Zones - 5 to 9

Height - 1 to 1.5 feet

Spread - 1 to 2 feet

Spacing - Plant in groups of two to three, 18 to 20 inches apart.

Exposure – Needs full sun or very light shade. It will not tolerate deep shade.

Soil - Feverfew grows best in a well-drained soil rich in humus.

Bloom time - mid-June–early July

Care - Feverfew is easy to maintain but watch out for seedlings that will self-generate. It has no serious pest problems. Dividing is rarely needed. Water moderately and do not water late in the day.

Chrysanthemum parthenium spp.

Creating a Deer-Proof G

Chrysanthemum superbum
Shasta Daisy

Description - Shasta daisy is an easy-to-grow plant with a tremendous amount of daisylike flowers at the end of multi branched stems. The flowers are about 2 to 3 inches in size and a bright white with bright yellow centers. I find the flower to be always attractive. They look very much like typical daisy's but are bigger in size. Shasta daisy is highly valued for its long bloom time. In the northeast region, it will flower for a very long period, from mid June to the first frost. The foliage is dark green in color and small in size, although dense. The leaves are narrow shaped and about one inch long. Shasta daisy will grow in a dense, bushy manner, but stays relatively neat in form. It is a medium to large size perennial and works best toward the middle or back of a border. It is also excellent for a rock garden. It is also a great plant for cut flowers. For the best effect, plant Shasta daisy in groups of two to three plants.

Zones - 5 to 9

Height - 2 to 4 feet

Spread - 2.5 to 4.5 feet

Spacing -Plant in groups of two to three, 18 to 24 inches apart.

Exposure – Needs full sun or partial shade. It will not tolerate deep shade.

Soil - Shasta daisy grows best in a well-drained soil rich in humus. It will not tolerate soggy soils.

Bloom time - mid-June–first frost

Care – Shasta daisy is moderately easy to maintain, but a number of insects will feed on its foliage. It is subject to crown rot, leaf spot, and other diseases. Divide every other year to invigorate the plants. Water moderately and do not water late in the day.

Chrysanthemum superbum Snowcap

Cimicifuga racemosa
Bugbane

Description - Bugbane is a native woodland plant that grows naturally at the forest edge. It produces very long spikes or spires with attractive white flowers sitting on top. The flowers are tiny but bloom in a profuse manner in spires that can be 6 feet higher than the foliage! The flowers are always white and give off a faint scent. The foliage is dark green, has a jagged edge, and stays attractive until frost. The white flowers contrasting against the dark green foliage creates a nice look. Bugbane grows in a clump form. It is not considered invasive as it grows slowly. It is fairly easy to grow and has no serious pest problems. It is a medium-size perennial, but because of the very tall flowering spikes, it works best in the back of the border. For the best effect, plant as a lone specimen or in groups of two to three plants.

Zones - 3 to 8

Height - 2 to 3.5 feet (Flower stalks can be as high as 8 feet above the foliage clumps.)

Spread - 2 to 2.5 feet

Cimicifuga racemosa

Spacing - Plant in groups of one to two, 18 to 24 inches apart.

Exposure - Dappled shade is best. Bugbane will not tolerate more than three hours of full sun per day.

Soil - Bugbane grows best in a well-drained, moist soil that is rich in humus/organic matter.

Bloom time - mid-June–early July

Care - Bugbane is easy to maintain. It does need frequent fertilizing and deep watering. It has no serious pest problems. Dividing is rarely needed. Water moderately and do not water late in the day.

Coreopsis lanceolata
Coreopsis

Description - Coreopsis is yet another member of the daisy family. There are many different species of coreopsis; most have yellow flowers, but there are a few offering pink flowers. Coreopsis is fairly easy to grow and always attractive. The lancelolata species produces a tremendous amount of daisylike yellow flowers at the end of long stems. The flowers are about 2.5 inches in size and yellow with reddish brown or gold centers. Coreopsis is

Coreopsis lanceolata sterntaler

highly valued for its long bloom time, which will last from June through September. The foliage is dark green in color, narrow, elongated, and attractive. It is a small-size perennial, and because of it's height, it works best in the front of a border. It can also be used effectively in the rock garden. Coreopsis is not invasive and will always stay inbounds. For the best effect, plant coreopsis in groups of four to five plants.

Zones - 3 to 9

Height - 1.5 to 2 feet

Spread - 1 to 1.5 feet

Spacing - Plant in groups of four to five, 12 to 16 inches apart.

Exposure - full sun

Soil - Coreopsis grows best in a well-drained soil that is not overly rich.

Bloom time - mid-June–September

Care - Coreopsis requires frequent care; watch out for leaf spot, rust, and powdery mildew. It has no serious pests but is subject to a number of foliage-feeding insects. Division is needed every four years. Water moderately and do not water late in the day.

Coreopsis lanceolata **spp.**

Dianthus plumarius
Cottage Pinks

Description - Dianthus is a member of the pinks family, native to Scotland, with many different cultivars available. Pinks are a popular choice in numerous perennial gardens because of its ease of growth, and plentiful flower production. The flowers are small, about 1.5 inches in size and range in color from classic pink to rose, red, or white. A few varieties have multicolor flowers. The foliage is very attractive also, made of dense tufts of narrow grass like gray/green leaves. Pinks are small-size perennials working best in the front of the border.

They can be used very effectively in the rock garden as well. Dianthus is not invasive, always staying neat and compact. A great variety is rosie cheeks, which has softly colored pink flowers with contrasting red interiors. For the best effect, plant dianthus in groups of three to four plants.

Zones - 4 to 9

Height - 5 to 9 inches

Spread - 10 to 14 inches

Spacing - Plant in groups of three to four, 12 to 16 inches apart.

Exposure - full sun

Soil - Pinks grow best in a well-drained sandy soil that is not overly rich.

Bloom time - mid-May–June

Care - Pinks are easy to maintain but watch out for leaf spot and powdery mildew. Division is needed every four years. Water moderately and do not water late in the day.

Dianthus plumarius
Rosie Cheeks

Dianthus plumarius spp.

Dicentra spectabilis
Common Bleeding Heart

Description - Bleeding heart is a classic border perennial widely used in victorian times. It is known for its foot-long stems of heart-shaped pink and white hanging flowers. The flowers are about 1 inch in size and range in color from classic pink, to rose, or purple. White is also available. The foliage is lush with gray, green finely textured leaves, dying back in midsummer. Bleeding heart is a medium-size perennial that works best toward the middle of a border. It can be used effectively in the rock garden as well. It is relatively easy to grow but, generally, will die down after blooming, leaving bare spots after it blooms. To remedy this, plant annuals near the bare spots to fill in the barren areas. Bleeding heart is not invasive. For the best effect, plant bleeding heart in groups of two to three plants.

***Dicentra spectabilis* spp.**

Zones - 3 to 9

Height - 1.5 to 3 feet

Spread - 2.5 to 3 feet

Spacing - Plant in groups of one to two, 20 to 24 inches apart.

Exposure - partial shade

Soil - Bleeding heart grows best in a well-drained, rich soil that is high in organic matter.

Bloom time - mid-April–May

***Dicentra spectabilis* spp.**

Care - Bleeding heart can be difficult to maintain; it does not care for soggy/wet soils that are not quick draining. This will promote stem rot, which is the main problem with bleeding heart. Division is rarely needed and usually not successful. Water moderately and do not water late in the day.

Dictamnus albus
Gas Plant

Description - A member of the citrus family, native to Europe, gas plant is a shrubby perennial with a pungent lemon-oil-scented flower. The flowers are about 1 inch in size and range in color from pink, to light purple, to white. Individually, the flowers are quite small and unobtrusive, but they bloom in great quantities on spikes at the top of the plant. This creates a very attractive effect. The gas plant's foliage is extremely good-looking in its own right. It stays attractive until first frost in a glossy medium green color. Gas plant is a bushy and large perennial; it works best in the middle to rear of the border. It will be effective positioned as a specimen plant in an isolated corner or along a fence. Gas plant is known to spread at least 6 feet; give it room to grow. It is relatively easy to grow and long lived. Purpureus is an excellent cultivar with showy pink flowers.

For the best effect, plant gas plant in groups of one to three plants.

Zones - 3 to 8

Height - 3 feet

Spread - 5 to 6 feet

Spacing - Plant in groups of one to three, 36 inches apart.

Exposure - full sun or light, dappled shade

Soil – gas plant grows best in a well-drained soil that is rich in organic matter.

Bloom time - late May–June

Care - Gas plant is easy to maintain. It has no serious pest problems but does not respond to soggy/wet soils. Division is never needed. Gas plant does not respond to transplanting; be sure to plant it where it can grow for many years without disturbance. Water moderately and do not water late in the day.

Dictamnus albus purpureus

Dictamnus albus purpureus

Digitalis purpurea
Foxglove

Description - I find foxglove to be a dependable performer in my landscape beds. Although this plant is really a biennial and not a perennial, it self-sows so profusely that many experts treat it as a perennial in that it can be considered a permanent fixture in the garden. It is a member of the snapdragon family, native to the Mediterranean region. The flowers are about 2 to 2.5 inches in size and range in color from pink, to purple, to white, to red. There is even a yellow-flowering variety. The flowers are almost bell shaped and attractive individually, but they bloom in great quantities on spikes at the top of the plant. It makes a striking appearance. The flowers grow on tall spikes that can reach a height of 3 feet above the foliage. The foliage

Digitalis purpurea spp.

is somewhat attractive, but the star is the flowering spires located above the foliage. Each leave is dark green on the upper surface and light green beneath. The leaves seem to be much denser at the base of the plant and then become smaller and appear less frequently toward the top of the plant. After blooming, the foliage looses its attractiveness. Foxglove is a medium-to-large-size plant, and it works best positioned in the middle to the rear of a border. It can be used effectively as a specimen plant in an isolated corner or as an informal plant in a natural woodland setting. Foxglove is not considered invasive. It is relatively easy to grow. An interesting and unusual cultivar is giant shirley, which features a blend of purple, lavender, and white flowers. Another highly unusual flower is from pam's choice, which has white flowers with burgundy interiors. For the best effect, plant foxglove in groups of three to four plants.

Zones - 4 to 8

Height - 2 to 5 feet

Spread - 18 to 24 inches

Spacing - Plant in groups of three to four, 12 to 16 inches apart.

Digitalis Purpurea
Giant Shirley

Exposure - full shade or dappled shade

Soil- Foxglove grows best in a well-drained soil that is slightly acidic and rich in organic matter.

Digitalis purpurea
Pam's Choice

Bloom time - mid-June–July

Care - Foxglove is fairly easy to maintain. It has no serious pest problems but does not respond to soggy/wet soils. Division is never needed. Foxglove does not respond to transplanting. It is best to let the plants self-sow and then remove the entire plant. There can be occasional troubles with leaf spot, powdery mildew. Japanese beetles and aphids can be potential problems. Water moderately and do not water late in the day.

Echinacea puruprea
Purple Coneflower

Description - Purple coneflower is widely used in my perennial beds because of its many fine features. The flowers are daisylike and quite large, about 3 to 4 inches in size. They range in color from pink to light purple to white. The flowers are both striking and curious to look at. They have an unusual droop to them in that each petal droops back toward the stem rather than staying straight out. The foliage is also extremely attractive in its own right. It stays good-looking until the first frost,

Echinacea puruprea **spp.**

a pretty green color with finely cut lace-shaped leaves. Purple coneflower is a medium-to-large-size perennial, and it works best in the middle or the rear of a border. It can also be used effectively as a woodland plant at the wood's edge, where it grows naturally. It will also work well in a rock garden. Cornflower is an excellent choice for a natural wildflower meadow. Coneflower is not considered invasive. It is relatively easy to grow and long lived. It also makes an excellent cut flower. A great choice for this species is magnus. For the best effect, plant purple coneflower in groups of four to five plants.

Zones - 3 to 8

Height - 2 to 4 feet

Spread - 2 to 5 feet

Spacing - Plant in groups of four to five, 24 to 36 inches apart.

Exposure - full sun or light, dappled shade

Soil - Purple coneflower grows best in a well-drained soil that is slightly sandy. It grows naturally in prairies and in meadows, and in that setting, it will thrive.

Bloom time - late June–September

Echinacea puruprea magnus

Care - Purple cornflower is moderately easy to maintain. It does not respond to soggy/wet soils. Be aware of Japanese beetles, which will heavily feed on this plant. Division is needed every three to four years. Water moderately and do not water late in the day.

Echinops exaltus
Globe Thistle

Description - Globe thistle is a member of the daisy family although it looks or performs nothing like a daisy. The flowers are small individually but bloom in great profusion as a group in a sphere or globe shape about 2 inches in size. Valued for both its unusual shape of flower clusters and its long bloom season, globe thistle flowers come in various shades of blue or purple. The flowers are quite attractive and have an unusual, dramatic shape and effect to them. The foliage is extremely good-looking in its own right. It stays attractive until the first frost and is unusual in that it has a dark green color on the top of each leaf with white on the bottom. The finely cut leaves are toothed and have an interesting effect. Globe thistle is a medium-size perennial and works best in the middle or the rear of a border. It can also be used effectively as an individual plant in a rock garden. It also is an excellent choice for a natural wildflower meadow. Globe thistle is not considered invasive. It is relatively easy to grow and long lived. It also makes an excellent cut flower. For the best effect, plant globe thistle in groups of three to four plants.

Echinops

Zones - 3 to 8

Height - 3 to 4 feet

Spread - 18 to 24 inches

Spacing - Plant in groups of three to four, 24 inches apart.

Exposure -full sun or light, dappled shade

Soil - Globe thistle grows best in a well-drained soil that is slightly sandy with average fertility. It will not tolerate wet or soggy soils.

Bloom time - late June–August

Care - Globe thistle is easy to maintain. It does not respond at all to soggy/wet soils. It has no major pest problems. Division is needed every three to four years. Water moderately and do not water late in the day.

Echinops ritro

Euphorbia epithymoides
Cushion Spurge

Description - Cushion spurge is an unusual plant that always adds an element of drama to a garden. It is a member of the spurge family, native to Eastern Europe. The flowers are small individually and insignificant, but the stars are the showy yellow or purple bracts. Certain varieties are available in a reddish-colored flower also, but the most popular flower color choice is yellow. Cushion spurge is valued for its unusual, neat rounded growing habit. The foliage stays attractive all season; they are a deep green color during the growing season and in the fall turn a spectacular reddish color until first frost. Spurge is a small-sized perennial, and it works best in the front of a border. In my opinion, it is best as a lone specimen plant as it can spread invasively. It is an excellent choice for a rock garden. Spurge is relatively easy to grow as it tolerates a number of different soils types, drought, and neglect. It is also a long-lived plant.

Zones - 4 to 11

Height - 10 to 20 inches

Spread - 10 to 16 inches

Spacing - Plant as specimen, and plant in groups with 18 inches space between plants.

Exposure - full sun

Soil - Cushion spurge grows best in a well-drained soil with average fertility. It will grow in any type of soil, but note that in wet and rich soil, it could spread invasively.

Bloom time - late April–early June

Care - Cushion spurge is very easy to maintain. It is extremely tolerant of drought, neglect, and is pest free. Division is needed every two to three years. Water moderately and do not water late in the day.

Euphorbia epithymoides
Golden Tower

Filipendula rubra
Queen of the Prairie

Description - Queen of the prairie is a member of the rose family although it looks or performs nothing like a rose. It is a native plant, growing naturally in open meadows. Queen of the prairie flowers are formed in unusual clusters of tiny five-petal light pink plumes. The flowers are small individually but bloom in great profusion as a group in a feathery plume shape. The flowers will remind many of astilbe flowers. Queen of the prarie foliage is extremely attractive on its own, staying handsome until the first frost. Each leave is medium green in color and angular shaped. The plant itself is striking in that it grows in neat manner but grows rather tall. It is valued for both its unusual flowers and its height. It is a large perennial; it works best in the rear of a border. It also is an excellent choice for a natural wildflower meadow, which is its natural growing environment. Queen of the prairie is not considered invasive. It is relatively easy to grow and long lived. For the best effect, plant queen of the prairie in groups of two to three plants.

Filipendula rubra spp.

Zones - 3 to 9

Height - 5 to 6 feet

Spread - 18 to 24 inches

Filipendula rubra spp.

Spacing -Plant in groups of two to three, 26 inches apart.

Exposure - Full sun is best, but it will tolerate partial shade.

Soil - Queen of the prairie grows best in a well-drained soil that is slightly rich with organic matter, but it will also grow in wet, boggy soils.

Bloom time - late June–July

Care - Queen of the prairie is fairly easy to maintain. It has no major pest problems. Mildew may present a problem in very wet or humid conditions, but it can be controlled by a fungicide. Division is rarely needed, but it is an excellent way to increase plants. Water moderately and do not water late in the day.

Geum
Avens

Description - This striking plant is a member of the rose family. There are many species of avens available all with beautiful flower colors. Avens produce loose clusters of flowers that are small, about 1 inch in size but come in vivid, rich colors of orange, red, or yellow. Avens is highly prized for both the unusual colors of the flowers and its long bloom time. It can flower from May to August if spent flowers are removed before seed can set. The foliage is slightly fuzzy and grows in clumps of deep green leaves, nothing extraordinary; the stars are the flowers, not the foliage. Avens is a medium-size plant and works best in the middle of a border. It can also be used effectively as an individual plant in a rock garden. Avens is not considered invasive as it is a slow grower. It also makes an excellent cut flower. For the best effect, plant avens in groups of three to four plants.

Zones - 4 to 7

Height - 1 to 2.5 feet

Spread - 14 to 20 inches

Spacing - Plant in groups of three to four, 18 inches apart.

Exposure - full sun

Soil - Avens grows best in a well-drained soil that is slightly rich. It will not tolerate wet or soggy soils.

Bloom time - late May–August

Care - Avens are fairly difficult to maintain. They do not respond at all to soggy, wet soils or heavy clay soils. They have no major pest problems, but a few insect species will feed on it. Division is needed every three to four years. It is important to remove spent flower heads to promote a longer blooming period.

Geum spp

Geum
Mrs. Bradshaw

Gypsophila paniculata
Baby's Breath

Description - Certainly a perennial that will be recognized by everyone who sees it, baby's breath is a member of the pink family. Native to Eastern Europe, it is a favorite for cut flowers and arrangements. It is often used as a focal point in the middle of a border. Baby's breath flowers are quite tiny but bloom in tremendous profusion and create an airy effect. Generally, the flower color is white, but there are several varieties with a pink cast. The flowers completely cover the plant in July and can last until September if spent flowers are pinched. The foliage is a light grayish/green color that is not noticeable or remarkable. The foliage is dense from top to bottom, stays attractive all season, and grows in a neat rounded format. Baby's breath is not invasive. It is not demanding to grow as it has no serious pest problems and requires very little attention. Regular fertilizing and regular watering will promote strong growth. It is a medium-size perennial, and it works best in the middle of a border or in a rock garden.

For the best effect, plant baby's breath in groups of three to four plants.

Zones - 3 to 9

Height - 2 to 3 feet

Spread - 24 to 36 inches

Spacing - Plant in groups of three to four, 30 inches apart.

Exposure - full sun or partial shade

Soil - Baby's breath grows best in a well-drained soil that is not overly rich and typical garden soil.

Bloom time - July

Care - Baby's breath is fairly easy to maintain. It has no serious pest problems. Baby's breath may need stalking to prevent the tops from flopping over. Dividing is rarely needed as it is not invasive. It does not like excessively wet/soggy soils. Water moderately and do not water late in the day.

Gypsophila paniculata
Bristol Fairy

Iris pseudacorus
Water Flag Iris

Description - There are literally hundreds of iris cultivars available today. Unfortunately, only one cultivar that I know of is not devoured by deer, that being the water flag iris.

Water flag iris is a large, beardless iris that prefers a wet and boggy soil. It will not fair well in normal garden soil; it needs a moist soil to thrive. I planted this cultivar ten years ago alongside my pond, and they have self-sowed terrifically. Today the entire side of the pond is covered in a blaze of yellow flowers during the early spring. Water flag iris produces only yellow flowers, which bloom together in great abundance sitting atop three-foot-tall stems. Each flower is about 4 inches in size and together create a very striking display. The foliage is a very attractive, sword-shaped leaf with a medium green color. I find this plant to be good-looking through the entire growing season. The best use for water flag iris is alongside a stream or a pond or in naturally moist/boggy soil, where it can spread.

Zones - 3 to 8

Height - 42 inches

Spread - 24 inches

Spacing - Plant in groups of six to eight, 24 inches apart

Exposure - partial shade

Soil - Water flag iris grows best in a moist soil that is not overly acidic.

Bloom time - end March–April

Care - Water flag iris is very easy to maintain if planted in the right location. It has no serious pest problems. It will spread over time; give it room to spread out

Iris pseudacorus spp

Iris pseudacorus spp.

Helleborus niger
Christmas Rose

Description - Christmas rose is a member of the buttercup family, native to Europe. Not related to roses at all, this evergreen perennial can bloom in winter, given the right conditions. The flowers are generally white with a blush of pink. Each flower is from 3 to 4 inches in size, and all have yellow centers.

The foliage is a dark green color that is glossy, but it is not attractive. Christmas rose is not invasive; however, it can also be demanding to grow. It is a small-to-medium-size perennial and works best in the front or the middle of a border or in a rock garden. For the best effect, plant Christmas rose in groups of two to three plants.

Zones - 4 to 9

Height - 16 inches

Spread - 24 inches

Spacing - Plant in groups of two to three, 18 inches apart.

Exposure - full shade or partial shade

Soil - Christmas rose grows best in a well-drained, moist soil that is not overly acidic.

Bloom time - can bloom in November given the right conditions or as late as March

Care - Christmas rose are difficult to maintain. They are very fussy about soil requirements. Frequent addition of lime

Helleborus niger spp.

is necessary to keep the soil sweet. It does not respond well to fertilizer, however, as it may burn the sensitive roots. Leaf spot can be troublesome. A number of insect species feed upon it. Division is usually not successful; they resent disturbance. Water moderately and do not water late in the day.

Liatris spicata
Blazing Star, Gayfeather

Description - Blazing star is a member of the daisy family although it looks nothing like a daisy. Native to the eastern United States of America, blazing star is a prolific self-sower. Blazing star flowers are quite attractive and are usually a lavender or purple color. Some varieties are available with white flowers, but the best known flower color is purple or lavender. A great variety is kobold, which has a longer blooming period than others. Liatris flowers are tiny but bloom in great quantities along the upper 15 to 30 inches of the stems. Valued for the long blooming time, the flowers start blooming in July and will last until September. The foliage is almost grass-like in appearance; it is a dark green color, and the bottom leaves are much larger than the leaves at the top. In certain locations, it can border on being invasive. It will respond very well to wet meadows and marshes as this is its natural habitat. It is best used in a rock garden or as a specimen plant as it is too invasive for a border. Another good use is as a naturalized plant positioned alongside a pond or stream. Blazing star is not demanding to grow as it has no serious pest problems and requires very little attention. Regular fertilizing and regular watering will promote strong growth. For the best effect, plant blazing star in groups of two to three plants.

Zones - 3 to 19

Height - 2 to 5 feet

Spread - 18 to 26 inches

Spacing - Plant in groups of two to three,
18 inches apart.

Exposure - full sun

Soil - Blazing star grows best in a well-drained soil that is rich in organic matter and evenly moist.

Bloom time - July–September

Care - Blazing stars are very easy to maintain. Plant it knowing it can be invasive if planted in a location that it favors. It has no serious pest problems. Dividing is needed every four to five years. Water moderately and do not water late in the day.

Liatris spicata kobold

Liatris spicata

Lilium lancifolium
Tiger Lily

Description - Lilies are one of the oldest plant species in the world. Many cultivars are thousands of years old. There are a staggering number of lily varieties available, all quite beautiful. Unfortunately, only one variety that I know of that is deer proof, that being the tiger lily. This is the lily you see growing wild along the highways and country roads in rural areas. The flowers are very attractive, a bright orange color spotted with brown or purple dots. The flower size is a nice size, about 4 inches across, and they bloom from the middle of summer to the end of summer. Each flower lasts only one day. Tiger lily will multiply freely in a setting it likes and will form large clusters of plants over a period of time. Some of the best uses for tiger lily are as a naturalized plant in a woodland bed or in a perennial border.

Zones - 4 to 9

Height - 2 to 3 feet

Spread - 18 to 26 inches

Spacing - Plant in groups of four to five, 18 inches apart.

Exposure - full sun to slight shade

Soil - Tiger lilies grow best in a well-drained soil that is rich in organic matter and evenly moist.

Bloom time - July–September

Care - Tiger lily are very easy to maintain. It has no serious pest problems. Dividing is needed every four to five years. Water moderately and do not water late in the day.

Lilium lancifolium
Tiger Lilly

Lupinus
Russell Lupines

Description - Lupines are members of the pea family. A favorite for cut flowers and arrangements, it is often used as a focal point in the middle of a border. Individual Lupine flowers are pea shaped and come in colors from blues, to whites, to pinks, and to yellows. There are even bicolor varieties with two or more flower colors on each plant. The flowers grow in clusters that are up to 2 feet long and have a Popsicle shape creating a unique look. Lupines are very dramatic and showy. The foliage is dark green and dense. Each leave resembles a palm of a hand; they are quite striking and different. Lupines are large-size perennial and work best in the middle to the back of the border. They are not invasive. It should be noted that lupines are not easy to grow and require regular maintenance. The best variety, in my opinion, is Russell hybrids, which has multiple flower-color choices. For the best effect, plant lupines in groups of two to three plants.

Zones - 3 to 7

Height - 2.5 to 4.5 feet

Spread - 20 to 26 inches

Spacing - Plant in groups of two to three, 26 inches apart.

Exposure - full sun or partial shade

Soil - Lupines grow best in a well-drained soil that is not overly rich.

Bloom time - June

Care - Lupines can be difficult to maintain. They do not like hot summer climates preferring cooler, less humid climates. Lupines need regular insecticide and fungicide treatment to protect it from aphids, powdery mildew, and rust. Dividing is rarely needed. Water moderately and do not water late in the day.

Lupinus
Russell hybrids

Lupinus
Russell Hybrids

Lythrum salicaria
Purple Loosestrife

Description - I planted loosestrife alongside my pond, and it has added beauty and color to the setting. Loosestrife is a plant that grows tall and somewhat bushy with erect stems that produce many bright purple flowers all summer long. Its flowers are small, about one-half inch in size and range in color from pink or magenta to purple. The flowers completely cover the stems of the plant, which grow 4 to 5 feet above the foliage. They bloom in July and can last until September. A popular variety is firecandle, which is slightly less invasive and has larger flowers. Purple loosestrife foliage is a medium green color that is thin and attractive. It is a medium-to-large-size perennial and works best in the middle or a back of the border. I feel it may be better suited for a woodland setting, along a pond, or a place where it can spread such as a wildflower field. Purple loosestrife is considered invasive in certain settings. It likes wet areas along ponds, streams, etc.; and in those settings, it will reseed vigorously. It is not demanding to grow as it has no serious pest problems and requires very little attention. For the best effect, plant loosestrife in groups of two to three plants.

Lythrum salicaria spp.

Zones - 3 to 10

Height - 3 to 5.5 feet

Spread - 24 to 28 inches

Spacing - Plant in groups of two to three, 28 inches apart.

Exposure - partial shade to partial sun

Soil - Loosestrife grows best in a moist soil that is rich in organic matter, but it will perform well in normal garden soil.

Bloom time - July–September

Care - Loosestrife are very easy to maintain. It can be invasive in settings it favors. It has no serious pest problems. Dividing is rarely needed. Loosestrife does not like dry or sandy soils; it will survive in that setting but will not perform vigorously.

Lythrum salicaria
Firecandle

Monarda didyma
Bee Balm

Description - Bee balm is a member of the mint family, native to Eastern United States. Like all plants in the mint family, bee balm is avoided by deer. This is a plant that grows tall and somewhat bushy with erect stems that produce dense flowers. The flowers are highly attractive to bees, hummingbirds, and butterflies. Each flower are about 2 inches in size and come in a variety of colors from white, to pink, to purple, to red. The red-colored flowers are especially inviting to hummingbirds. A very nice red-flowering variety is Jacob Cline. Bee balm flowers will last a fairly long time, blooming in late June and lasting until August. The foliage is a dark green color that is thin and good-looking. Bee balm is considered invasive in certain settings. It thrives in shady areas that are rich in organic matter, and in that setting, it will spread vigorously. It

Monarda didyma
Jacob Cline

is not demanding to grow as it has no serious pest problems and requires very little attention. Bee balm is a medium-size perennial and works best in the middle of the border. It will also work well in a rock garden as a specimen. For the best effect, plant bee balm in groups of two to three plants.

Zones - 6 to 8

Height - 2 to 4 feet

Spread - 24 to 28 inches

Spacing -Plant in groups of two to three, 28 inches apart.
Exposure - partial shade to partial sun

Soil — Bee balm grows best in a moist soil that is rich in organic matter, but it will perform well in normal garden soil.

Bloom time - late June–August

Care - Bee balm are fairly easy to maintain. It has no serious pest problems. It can be prone to fungus problems such as powdery mildew if planted too close to each other in areas with poor air circulation. Division is needed every four years. Water moderately and do not water late in the day.

Monarda didyma
Blue Stocking

Narcissus
Daffodil

Description - Daffodils announce
the coming of spring with
spectacular flowers. There are
thousands of cultivars available,
and fortunately, all are deer proof!
Flowers bloom in late April and
will sometimes last until June.
There is a huge variety of flower
color choices from solid yellow,
to yellow with orange centers, to
white with orange centers. Daffodil
will work very well in a rock garden
as a specimen plant or in a formal
border. Some people simply take a
handful of bulbs and throw them
on their lawn or wildflower meadow
to create a natural look. Over time,
the bulbs will multiply and spread,
and each spring, a dense area of
flowering daffodil will appear.
Daffodil thrives in areas that are
rich in organic matter, and in that
setting, it will spread vigorously. It is
not demanding to grow as it has no
serious pest problems and requires
very little attention. For the best effect, plant daffodil
in groups of six to eight plants.

Narcissus **spp.**

Zones - 5 to 9

Height - 1 to 2 feet

Spread - 12 to 24 inches

Spacing - Plant in groups of six to eight, 24
inches apart.

Exposure - partial shade to partial sun

Soil - Daffodil grows best in a moist soil that is rich
in organic matter, but it will perform well in normal
garden soil. It does not tolerate soggy or overly
wet soils.

Bloom time - late April–June

Narcissus **spp.**

Care - Daffodils are very easy to maintain. It has no
serious pest problems. Division is needed every four
years. Water moderately and do not water late in the day.

Nepeta
Catmint, Catnip

Description - Catmint is a member of the mint family, native to Europe. Like all members of the mint family this plant is avoided by deer. Catmint is a plant that grows tall and somewhat bushy with upright stems producing many bright purple flowers from mid to late summer. Its flowers are small, about one-half inch in size and range in color from magenta, to pink, to purple. The flowers completely cover the stems of the plant, making a dramatic statement. The foliage is a medium gray or green color with thin leaves. Each leaf has a mint aroma. Catmint is a medium-size perennial and works best in the middle of the border. I find it works best in a woodland setting, along a pond, or a place where it can spread such as a wildflower field. A nice variety for blue/purple-colored flowers is blue wonder. Catmint is not considered invasive. It is not demanding to grow as it has no serious pest problems and requires very little attention. For the best effect, plant catnip in groups of two to three plants.

Zones - 3 to 8

Height - 2 to 3 feet

Spread - 24 to 28 inches

Spacing - Plant in groups of two to three, 28 inches apart.

Exposure - full sun to partial shade

Soil - Catmint grows best in a well-drained average garden soil.

Bloom time - late June–August

Care - Catmint are very easy to maintain. It has no serious pest problems. Dividing is rarely needed. Prune back after flowering to maintain vigorous growth and a second bloom. Water moderately and do not water late in the day.

Nepeta
Blue Wonder

Oenothera
Sundrops

Description - A member of the primrose family, native to the Midwestern United States, sundrops is a plant that grows small and in a trailing effect. Its flowers are large, about 4 to 5 inches in size and are a striking yellow color. The flowers last only one day but bloom in such profusion that the plant will stay in flower from early spring to summer. Sundrops foliage is a dark green color with thin leaves that stay attractive all season. It is a small-size perennial and works very well in the front of a border. Sundrops is not considered invasive. A great cultivar is silver wings, which has slightly variegated leaves and bright yellow flowers. For the best effect, plant sundrops in groups of four to five plants.

Zones - 5 to 9

Height - 12 to 15 inches

Spread - 24 to 28 inches

Spacing - plant in groups of four to five, 22 inches apart

Exposure - full sun

Soil - Sundrops grow best in a dry soil that is not rich in organic matter.

Bloom time - May–July

Care - Sundrops are very easy to maintain; it has no serious pest problems. Dividing is rarely needed. They do not like wet or soggy soils. Water moderately and do not water late in the day.

Oenothera spp.
Silver Wings

Papaver orientales
Oriental poppy

Description - I use poppy in every perennial bed I plant in. A member of the poppy family, native to Asia, this is one of the world's most popular perennials. It is a well-behaved plant that never grows out of its boundaries and is never invasive. The striking and vivid flower colors are very dramatic and showy. Poppy flowers are large, about 4 to 5 inches in size with some varieties having a nine-inch flower! The original poppy flower color was a bright orange color. Now, there are varieties available with pink, white, or red flowers. Still in all, the most famous and largely used flower color is the species with the

***Papaver orientales* spp.**

orange flowers. If you are looking for something different, try a pink-flowering variety such as pink ruffles. Another great variety with the typical red/orange flower color is named turkenlouis. Many poppy flowers have a black center, giving a nice contrast to each bloom. The foliage is a light green/gray color with leaves that are large and slightly hairy. Generally, the foliage will die down in August and may reappear again in September depending on the species. It is a medium-to-large-size perennial, and because of its height, it works very well in the middle or rear of the border. It is also widely used in rock gardens as a specimen plant. Poppy is not considered invasive. For the best effect, plant poppies in groups of four to five plants.

Zones - 3 to 7

Height - 2 to 4 feet

Spread - 30 to 36 inches

Spacing - Plant in groups of three to four, 18 inches apart.

Exposure - full sun or partial shade

Soil - Poppy grows best in a well-drained soil that is not too rich in organic matter. Average garden soil is best. It is important that the soil drains fairly quickly.

Bloom time - June

Care - Poppy is not the easiest plant to grow. It can be very finicky about soil requirements; it will not tolerate wet crowns and overly soggy soil. Do not let water stand on its foliage as it promotes fungus. Aphids can be a real problem. Division is needed every four years. Water moderately and do not water late in the day.

Papaver orientales
Pink Ruffles

Papaver orientales
Turkenlouis

Platycodon grandiflorus
Balloon Flower

Description - The balloon flower is a popular perennial, whose name aptly describes its blossoms. When the flower is in bud, the buds resemble inflated balloons, creating an unusual effect. The flowers are about 3 to 4 inches in size, have a cupped effect, and five pointed lobes. They are usually blue; however, there are varieties available now with pink or white flowers, but blue is the most popular color. The flowers resemble morning glory flowers in shape and size and will bloom in July and often lasting until September. The flowers are interspersed on top of each stem and also within the foliage, so there are flowers halfway down the plant as well. The foliage is a very attractive medium green color with a bluish cast to the underside of the leaves. Each leaf is about 2 inches in size and have an narrow elongated shape. Balloon flower stays bushy from top to bottom and will grow to 3 feet tall. It is not considered invasive, and it is long lived and easy to care for. A great variety with striking powder blue flowers is Fuji blue. Balloon flower is a medium-size perennial and works well in the middle of the border. For the best effect, plant balloon flower in groups of two to three plants.

Zones - 3 to 8

Height - 2 to 3 feet

Spread - 18 inches

Platycodon grandiflorus
Fuji Blue

***Platycodon grandiflorus* spp.**

Spacing - Plant in groups of two to three, 20 inches apart.

Exposure - full sun or partial shade

Soil - Balloon flower grows best in a well-drained soil that is slightly sandy, allowing for good drainage and not too rich in organic matter.

Bloom time - July–September

Care - Balloon flower are very easy to maintain. It has no serious pest problems. Dividing is rarely, if ever, needed. It does not like overly wet or soggy soils, especially in winter. Water moderately and do not water late in the day.

Primula vulgaris
English Primrose

Description - Primrose is an extremely large genus of plants with several hundred species, mostly native to Europe. There is a huge variance in each species as some will grow only to 3 inches while others will grow over 3 feet! Generally, primrose foliage will be in the form of crinkled rosettes that are sometimes evergreen. English primrose flowers are generally yellow, but there are varieties available now with pink and purple flowers. Its flowers are about 1 inch in size and completely cover the stems of the plant while blooming profusely. Primrose is a small-to-medium-size perennial, and it works best in the front or middle of the border. It will also work well in a rock garden. Primrose is not considered invasive. It is not demanding to grow as it has no serious pest problems and requires very little attention. For the best effect, plant primrose in groups of two to three plants.

Zones - 3 to 8

Height - 3 inches to 3 feet

Spread - 6 to 15 inches

Spacing - Plant in groups of two to three, 20 inches apart.

Exposure - full sun

Soil - Primrose grows best in a well-drained average garden soil.

Bloom time - late April–June

Care - Primrose are moderately easy to maintain. It has no serious pest problems, but slugs and snails can be present. Dividing is needed every three years. Water moderately and do not water late in the day.

Primula vulgaris **spp.**

Pulmonaria saccharata
Lungwort, Bethlehem Sage

Description - An interesting perennial that is used more as a ground cover with attractive bell-shaped flowers. Lungwort flowers are generally one-half inch in size and come in blue, white, red, or pink depending on the species. The foliage is unusual and attractive; it is variegated with dark green leaves that are mottled with white or, sometimes, yellow. Each leave is about 6 inches long and is heart shaped. Lungwort is a small-size perennial, and because of its low height, it works best in the front of a border. It will also work well in a rock garden as a specimen. Lungwort is not considered invasive. It is not demanding to grow as it has no serious pest problems and requires very little attention. For the best effect, plant lungwort in groups of four to five plants.

Zones - 3 to 10

Height - 5 to 9 inches

Spread - 8 to 10 inches

Spacing - Plant in groups of four to five, 10 inches apart.

Exposure - partial to full shade

Soil - Lungwort grows best in a well-drained, moist soil rich with organic matter.

Bloom time - late April–May

Care - Lungwort are very easy to maintain. It has no serious pests, but slugs and snails can present problems. It does not like dry, sandy areas. Division is rarely required. Water moderately and do not water late in the day.

Pulmonaria saccharata
British Sterling

Salvia × Superba and Salvia splendens
Perennial Salvia

Description - There are many, many cultivars of perennial salvia. In my opinion, the two best cultivars are x superba and splendens; they are more restrained in growth than the other cultivars and produce more flowers. I widely use salvia in my landscape because of its ease to grow and its long bloom period. Salvia is member of the mint family, native to Europe. Like all species in the mint family, salvia is totally avoided by deer. It is a popular perennial because of its good-looking foliage, interesting flower spikes, and the long bloom time of the flowers. Salvia flowers are very small individually but bloom in great profusion along six-inch spikes. Flower colors are available in deep purple, white, or red. The foliage is a medium green color and grows in pairs along square stems. Overall, it spreads slowly to form dense clumps. Salvia is a medium-size perennial, and it works best in the middle of a border. It will also work very well in a rock garden. Salvia is not considered invasive. It is

not demanding to grow as it has no serious pest problems and requires very little attention. For the best effect, plant salvia in groups of three to four plants. Plant the grouping in the same color for the most impact.

Zones - 4 to 7

Height - 2 to 3 feet

Spread - 1 to 2 feet

Spacing - Plant in groups of three to four, 18 inches apart.

Exposure - full sun

Soil - Salvia grows best in a well-drained soil rich with organic matter.
Bloom time - late June–July

Salvia Splendens
Vista Red

Care - Salvia are easy to maintain. It has no serious pests, but whitefly can be a minor problem. Remove spent flowers to prolong bloom period. Salvia does not like wet or soggy soils. Division is rarely required. Water moderately and do not water late in the day.

***Salvia* x *superba* spp.**

Solidago hybrids
Goldenrod

Description - Goldenrod is an interesting perennial with bright yellow flowers and is valued for its late bloom period. In the last fifty years, goldenrod has had a negative and unjustified reputation as a promoter of hay fever. In fact, it does not promote hay fever as its pollen is carried by insects and is not airborne. It is the ragweeds flowers that bloom at the same time as goldenrod that are the cause of hay fever. Goldenrod flowers are tiny, generally only one-eight inches in size and only to be had in yellow. They bloom in great profusion along flower stalks that grow out from the stems. The foliage is attractive with medium lance-shaped green leaves. Goldenrod is a medium-size perennial, and it works best in the middle of a border. It will also work well in a rock garden or a wildflower meadow, where it can naturalize freely. Goldenrod is not considered invasive. It is not demanding to grow as it has no serious pest problems and requires very little attention. For the best effect, plant goldenrod in groups of three to four plants.

Zones - 5 to10

Height - 16 to 36 inches

Spread - 12 to 16 inches

Spacing - Plant in groups of three to four, 13 inches apart.

Exposure - full sun
Soil - Goldenrod grows best in a well-drained, moist soil rich with organic matter.

Bloom time - late August–September

Care - Goldenrod are very easy to maintain. It has no serious pest problems. Goldenrod does not like overly dry or overly wet soils. A typical garden soil will do fine. Division is rarely required. Water moderately and do not water late in the day.

Solidago
Gold Rush

Stachys byzantina
Lamb's Ear

Description - Lamb's ear is a member of the mint family, native to Turkey. Like all species in the mint family, lamb's ear is totally avoided by deer. An interesting plant, it is used as both a ground cover and as a low-growing perennial in the flowerbed. It has small but good-looking flowers held on twelve-inch spikes; however, lamb's ear is grown more for its foliage than its flowers. The foliage is handsome in that the leaves are dense, wooly, or slightly hairy and have soft silver cast to them. Many people mix lamb's ear foliage with flowering perennials that have shades of blue and pink flowers for an eye-catching accent.

Stachys byzantina spp.

These flower colors contrast nicely against the silver foliage of lamb's ear foliage. Lamb's ear is a small-size perennial, and it works best in the front of a border. It will also work well in a rock garden. Lamb's ear is not considered invasive. It is not demanding to grow as it has no serious pest problems and requires little attention. For the best effect, plant lamb's ear in groups of three to four plants.

Zones - 4 to 8

Height - 6 to 11 inches

Spread - 26 inches

Spacing - Plant in groups of three to four, 18 inches apart.

Exposure - full sun

Soil - Grows best in a well-drained soil not too rich with organic matter.

Bloom time - late July–August

Care - Lamb's ear are fairly easy to maintain. It has no serious pest problems. Lamb's ear does not like wet or soggy areas. Division is required every three to four years. Water moderately and do not water late in the day.

Verbascum
Nettle-Leaved Mullein,

Description - A member of the snapdragon family, native to Greece, mullein is a stately plant-bearing columns of five-petal flowers. Mullein flowers are generally one-half inch in size, available in yellow, white, pink, or apricot. Flowers bloom at the same time along upright flower stalks, creating a very pleasing and showy effect. The foliage is highly attractive in its own right with wooly or slightly hairy dark green leaves that grow densely together. Mullein is a large-size perennial working best in the back of a border. It will also work well in a wildflower meadow or in a rock garden. Mullein is not considered invasive. It is not demanding to grow as it has no serious pest problems and requires little attention. Jackie is an excellent variety with softly colored peach flowers. For the best effect, plant mullein in groups of two to three plants.

Zones - 4 to 8

Height - 5 to 6 feet
Spread - 2.5 to 3 feet

Spacing - Plant in groups of two to three, 24 inches apart.

Exposure - full sun

Soil - Mullein grows best in a well-drained, sandy soil with average fertility.

Bloom time - July–August

Care - Mullein are easy to maintain. It has no serious pest problems. Mullein does not like wet or soggy areas. Division is rarely required. Water moderately and do not water late in the day.

Verbascum phoeniceum
Jackie

Verbascum phoeniceum
Jackie

Yucca
Adam's Needle

Description - A native plant to the southwestern United States of America, yucca is a dramatic plant that creates an interesting effect in the right setting. I use Adam's needle extensively, and it never fails to add a unique look to its location. Although Adam's needle is grown primarily for its foliage, which creates a southwestern look, the flowers are very attractive. Each flower is 2 inches long, solid white, and sort of bell shaped. They grow along a tall center flower stalk that grows 3 feet tall, standing 2 feet above the plant. It is a very unique and attractive look. Each stalk will hold dozens of flowers. The foliage is attractive and evergreen. Each leave grows 2 feet or more and is spine tipped. Some varieties are available with variegated foliage, creating even more drama. Yucca is a large-size perennial, and it works best in the back of a border. It will also work very well in a rock garden. I like it as a stand-alone plant softening a corner in a shrub bed. Yucca is not considered invasive. It is not demanding to grow as it has no serious pest problems and requires very little attention. For the best effect, plant yucca in groups of one to two plants.

Zones - 4 to 9

Height - 5 to 8 feet

Spread - 3 to 6 feet

Spacing - Plant in groups of one to two, 36 inches apart.

Exposure - Full sun is best but will tolerate partial shade.

Soil - Yucca grows best in a well-drained, sandy soil not too rich with organic matter.

Bloom time - late June–July

Care - Yucca are very easy to maintain. It has no serious pest problems. They do not like soggy areas; plant in a normal garden soil making sure it has good drainage. Division is rarely required. Water moderately and do not water late in the day.

Yucca filamentosa
Golden Sword

Other Deer-Proof Perennials

Ornamental Grasses and Ferns

The following plants, while not flowering perennials, are an important ingredient in any landscape and should be considered in yours. There are many, many, different species of ornamental grasses and ferns available today. I have listed, in my opinion, only the best landscape plants from this group, plants that offer at least two to three seasons of interest and that are not overly invasive.

Ornamental Grasses

Arrhenatherum elatius var. *bulbosum* "Variegatum"
Variegated Bulbous Oat Grass

A highly attractive grass that is grown for its distinctive striped green and white leaves, it is bold in its appearance and adds a certain brightness to any shady spot. Unfortunately, it can be invasive in rich soils and will quickly takeover a bed. I situated this grass in slightly boggy, wet soil alongside a pond, which slows its growth. It is also in a semi- shaded location. It is very content there and stays inbounds. Care should be taken in giving thought to where to plant this species. It can be troublesome in terms of invasiveness yet it is a beautiful plant. Situate it in the right location, and it will work fine.

Zones - 5 to 9

Height - 3 to 4 feet

Spread - indefinite

Spacing - Plant in groups of two to three, 36 inches apart.

Exposure - Full sun is best but will tolerate partial shade.

Soil - Oat grass grows best in a well-drained, sandy soil not too rich with organic matter. To control its growth, plant in a heavy/boggy soil in semishade.

Care - Oat grass are very easy to maintain. It has no serious pest problems. Water moderately and do not water late in the day.

Arrhenatherum elatius var. bulbosum

Calamagrostis epigeous hortorum
Reed Grass

A widely used grass grown for its neat vertical effect, it is striking when in flower during July with golden spikes that stay handsome all through the winter. This is one of the few grasses that prefer a boggy, wet soil, and in that setting, it may quickly establish itself faster than you may want. It will do quite nicely planted in average garden soil in a sunny spot.

Zones - 6 to 9

Height - 3 to 6 feet

Spread - 3 to 4 feet

Spacing - plant as a specimen

Exposure - Full sun is best but will tolerate partial shade.

Soil - Reed grass grows best in a well-drained soil not too rich with organic matter.

Care - Reed grass are very easy to maintain. It has no serious pest problems. Water moderately and do not water late in the day.

Calamagrostis

Deschampsia caespitosa
Tufted Hair Grass

Another widely used grass grown for its rounded mounding effect, the flowers are inconspicuous; it is the mounding shape that makes this plant desirable. It is very easy to grow as it tolerates sun or shade and moist or dry soil. Tufted hair grass is not considered invasive. It will grow quite nicely in average garden soil in a sunny spot.

Zones - 6 to 9

Height - 3 feet

Spread - 2 to 3 feet

Spacing - plant as a specimen

Exposure - Full sun is best but will tolerate partial shade

Soil - Tufted hair grass grows best in a well-drained soil not too rich with organic matter.

Care - Tufted hair grass are very easy to aintain. It has no serious pest problems. Water moderately and do not water late in the day.

Deschampsia caespitosa

Festuca ovina var. *glauca*
Dwarf Blue Fescue

An extremely popular plant noted for its blue foliage, which is very dramatic and showy.
It is my favorite grass species as I love the striking blue color, which contrasts with its neighboring green plants.
Dwarf blue fescue grows in a compact mounding form. It stays small, growing only up to 1 foot tall. Blue fescue
is widely used as edging along a border or walkway. Another good use is as a specimen in a rock garden. It will
grow well in average garden soil in either a sunny spot or a slightly shady location.

Zones - 4 to 9

Height - 8 to 12 inches

Spread - 2 feet

Spacing - 18 inches apart or plant as a specimen

Exposure - Full sun is best but will tolerate partial shade.

Soil - Dwarf blue fescue grows best in a well-drained soil not too rich with organic matter.

Care - Dwarf blue fescue are very easy to maintain. It has no serious pest problems. Blue fescue may need
division every few years to keep the centers of the clumps from dying out. Water moderately and do not water
late in the day.

Festuca Glauca

Miscanthus sinensis
Eulalia Grass

This is another popular grass widely used for its vertical growth, which bends slightly at the top. It is very graceful in appearance, but it does grow quite tall. Eulalia grass will grow from 5 to 11 feet tall and should be planted with care if there are concerns about height restrictions. The foliage is slender and changes to a goldish brown color that stays in color through the winter. It is very attractive during July when in flower, with six-inch plumes of feathery silver/white flowers. The flower plumes will stay all winter long. A popular use for eulalia grass is as specimen plant used for screening. Plant it along a fence for screening, to screen out pool equipment, etc. Eulalia grass will grow well in average garden soil in a sunny spot.

Zones - 4 to 9

Height - 5 to 11 feet

Spread - 4 to 5 feet

Spacing - 5 feet apart or plant as a specimen

Exposure - Full sun is best but will tolerate partial shade.

Soil - Eulalia grass grows best in a well-drained soil not too rich with organic matter.

Care - Eulalia grass are very easy to maintain. It has no serious pest problems. Water moderately and do not water late in the day.

Miscanthus sinensis spp.

Miscanthus sinensis spp.
Summer Flowers

Pennisetum alopecuroides
Fountain Grass

Fountain grass is a species widely used for its dramatic plumes of flowers. They spray out in an arching effect covering the entire plant in summer, giving it a fountain effect. Fountain grass stays relatively small in growth, only growing to about 3 feet tall. The foliage is very slender and fine. In fall, the foliage changes to an attractive yellow color. Overall, it is very graceful in appearance and stays inbounds. Fountain grass is a solid choice as specimen plant used in a rock garden or in a border. It will grow well in average garden soil in full sun.

Zones – 6 to 9

Height - 3 feet

Spread - 3 to 4 feet

Spacing - 4 feet apart or plant as a specimen

Exposure - Full sun is best, but it will tolerate partial shade.

Soil - Fountain grass grows best in a well-drained soil not too rich with organic matter.

Care - Fountain grass are very easy to maintain. It has no serious pest problems. Water moderately and do not water late in the day.

Pennisetum alopecuroides spp.

Phalaris
Ribbon Grass

Another variegated grass that has recently grown in popularity. It has very dramatic variegated foliage that is striped green and white. It can brighten up a dark area, but there is a down side; it can also spread invasively in the right growing conditions. For this reason, I am a not a big fan of ribbon grass. It spreads by underground runners and can be difficult to remove after establishing growth. It can be contained more readily by planting it in heavy clay soil that is wet. Alongside a pond or a stream is perfect. Under these conditions ribbon grass will stay inbounds. The foliage is sword shaped, with slender leaves. In fall, the foliage changes to a brown color and can stay that way all winter. Plant ribbon grass as a highlight or accent in a rock garden or in a border. Many people use it as a backdrop to featured plants. Ribbon grass will grow well in average garden soil in a sunny spot.

Zones - 4 to 9

Height - 3 feet

Spacing - 4 feet apart or plant as a specimen

Exposure - Full sun is best but will tolerate partial shade.

Spread- indefinite

Soil - Ribbon grass grows best in a well-drained soil not too rich with organic matter. Plant it in heavy soil to slow its growth as it could become invasive.

Care - Ribbon grass are very easy to maintain. It has no serious pest problems. Be mindful of its tendency to spread invasively. Water moderately and do not water late in the day.

Phalaris spp.

Ferns

Ferns are an important landscape species widely used for ground cover or as specimens in a rock garden or border. Their greatest benefit is to add texture to any bed. The variety in terms of color choices and foliage of ferns will surprise you. Ferns prefer partial to full shade and need rich humus soils to thrive. All ferns will grow well as an under story plant under a canopy of trees or shrubs.

Adiantum
Maidenhair Fern

This is a very popular fern that is extremely delicate in appearance with finely textured foliage. The foliage is a beautiful bright green color that contrasts well with shrubs and flowers. Maidenhair fern spreads by creeping root stalks, but it is not a very fast spreader. Overall, it is very graceful in appearance and a nice addition to any garden. Maidenhair fern will grow only 4 feet wide, so it can be placed in a border and not take over the area. A popular use for maidenhair fern is as specimen plant in the rock garden or in the border.

Zones - 6 to 10

Height - 3 feet

Spread - 3 to 4 feet

Spacing - 4 feet apart or plant as a specimen

Exposure - Full sun is best but will tolerate partial shade

Soil - Maidenhair fern grows best in a well-drained soil not too rich with organic matter.

Care - Maidenhair fern are very easy to maintain. It has no serious pest problems. Water moderately and do not water late in the day.

Adiantum pedatum

Adiantum
Lady Fern, Japanese Painted Fern

This delicate looking and beautiful fern is my favorite fern species. There are two foliage choices. The Japanese painted fern is far more interesting than the lady fern in that its foliage color is a silver/green color that really stands out from a distance. The lady fern foliage color is a bright green that is also attractive, but this color can be found in other fern varieties. Both species always stay neat and compact and have great-looking foliage. The foliage is very finely cut, giving it a sculptured look almost reminiscent of Japanese maples. Both species are not invasive and grow relatively slowly by spreading rootstalks. Use them as a ground cover under a canopy or as specimen plants in an informal woodland garden or in a rock garden. These ferns will grow from 1 to 4 feet high, depending on the species.

Zones - 6-10

Height - 1 to 4 feet

Spacing - 3 feet apart or plant as a specimen

Exposure - Partial shade is best.

Soil - Japanese painted fern grows best in a well-drained soil that is slightly moist and rich with organic matter.

Care - Japanese painted fern are very easy to maintain. It has no serious pest problems. Water moderately and do not water late in the day.

Pictum
Japanese Painted Fern

Adiantum
Lady Fern

Polystichum
Shield Fern

This is a large group of native ferns growing naturally in the northeast. Chances are you already have this plant on your property, along the property edges. Shield ferns grow from 2 to 4 feet and spread slowly. They are best used as accent plant to compliment a woodland garden or in a rock garden. I do not recommend them as a ground cover as they will not cover large areas. Each species has nicely textured sword-shaped fronds that are a medium green color. It is not as finely sculptured or textured as some other ferns but still attractive in its own way.

Zones - 5 to 9

Height - 2 to 4 feet

Spacing - 4 feet apart or plant as a specimen

Exposure - full shade to partial shade.

Soil - Shield fern grows best in a well-drained soil that is slightly moist and rich with organic matter.

Care - Shield fern are very easy to maintain. It has no serious pest problems. Water moderately and do not water late in the day.

Polystichum
Polyblepharum

Deer-Proof Annuals

I will admit it; I am not a big lover of annuals. Many annuals are high maintenance—requiring fertilizing weekly, dead heading, insect removal, etc. All this for a plant that will only live four to six months. Next year, you get to do it all over again. Still in all, annuals do serve an important role in our landscape. I do begrudgingly use annuals in my home garden because they add color and interest to areas of our garden that need it. More importantly, many annuals bloom at a time when most flowering shrubs, tress, and perennials are finished blooming.

Many of the old favorites such as impatiens and pansies are *not* deer-proof and should be avoided at all cost; however, there are enough deer-proof annuals to keep any annual lover happy.

Ageratum
Floss Flower (Dwarf)

Description — A native to Mexico, this very popular and low-growing annual is great for edging. It also works well in a classic perennial bed. Ageratum flowers are quite small but bloom in great profusion from late spring to fall. The purple color of the flowers are always attractive when set against yellow-flowering background plants. That combination is a classic garden look and is very striking. Ageratum also comes in a white-flowering variety as well as a pink variety, but purple is, by far, the most popular color.

Height - 6 to 8 inches depending on the variety

Spread - 10 inches

Spacing - Plant in groups of six to seven, 10 inches apart.

Exposure - full sun or light, dappled shade

Soil - Ageratum grows best in a well-drained soil that is slightly rich.

Bloom time - late June–September

Care - Ageratum are easy to maintain. They do not respond to soggy or wet soils. Shear off the faded flower heads to promote more blooms. Water moderately and do not water late in the day.

Ageratum houstonianom
Blue Danube

Antirrhinum majus
Snapdragon

Description - A native to the Mediterranean region, this very popular annual is a great compliment to perennials as it blends seamlessly with perennials. The flowers are very attractive, come in a multitude of colors, and prized for their long blooming season. The lower-growing varieties are used for edging.

Height - 6 to 45 inches depending on the variety

Spread - 10 inches

Spacing - Plant in groups of four to five, 10 inches apart.

Exposure - full sun or light, dappled shade

Soil - Snapdragon grows best in a well-drained soil that is slightly rich.

Bloom time - late June–September

Care - Snapdragon are easy to maintain. They do not respond to soggy or wet soils. Pinch off faded flower heads to promote more blooms. Water moderately and do not water late in the day.

Antirrhinum majus spp

Antirrhinum majus
Yellow

Begonia semperflorens cultorum
Wax Begonia

Description - A native to Brazil, this extremely popular annual is prized for its long blooming season and its ability to grow in shade. They will also grow in full sun, but their real value is that they will brighten up shady areas. The flowers are small but bloom in plentiful quantities. Available color choices are white, red, or pink. The foliage is also attractive in that you will find varieties with either bronze or green foliage. Wax begonia is a very easy annual to grow, and that is why it seems like it is featured in every garden in America. Use wax begonia as an edging plant or in a mass. A classic combination is wax begonia with dusty miller as a background plant.

Height - 5 to 12 inches depending on the variety

Spread - 10 inches

Spacing - Plant in groups of six to seven, 10 inches apart.

Exposure - shade or partial sun

Soil - Begonia grows best in a well-drained soil that is slightly rich, but it will grow in any garden soil.

Bloom time - late May–first frost

Care - Begonia are very easy to maintain. Begonia does not respond to soggy or wet soils. Pinch off faded flower heads to promote more blooms. Water moderately and do not water late in the day.

Begonia semperflorens cultorum
Hybrids

Cleome hassleriana
Spider Flower

Description - A native to South America, this not very well-known annual should be more popular than it is. I suspect that its limited popularity is that it is not readily available in many nurseries. Based on its merits, spider flower should be a popular plant indeed. It has a very long bloom season—from May to the first frost; it grows in all soil types, grows upright and tall (3 to 6 feet), and it is not bothered by extreme heat and humidity. The flowers are very showy and appear as clouds above the foliage in colors such as white, red, or violet. Spider flower works well in a classic perennial bed, positioned toward the back. It is also valued for its excellent cut flowers.

Height - 3 to 6 feet

Spread - 36 inches

Spacing - Plant in groups of one to two, 36 inches apart.

Exposure - full sun or light, dappled shade

Soil - Spider flower grows best in a well-drained soil that is slightly rich.

Bloom time - late June–first frost

Care - Spider flower are easy to maintain. They do not respond to soggy or wet soils. Water moderately and do not water late in the day.

***Cleome hassleriana* spp.**

Dahlia hybrids
Dahlia

Description - Native to Central America, this spectacular bloomer is a favorite annual of many gardeners and for good reason. Dahlia comes in a wide variety of colors; in fact, the only color not available is blue! It has a relatively long bloom season (midsummer to frost), and it can be found in any size from 12 inches to 6 feet tall! The flowers are very showy and range in size from 1 inch to almost 10 inches across, depending on the variety. They can be had in both single- and double-flowering varieties. There are many types of dahlias available. Bedding dahlias will work well in the front of the border. Exhibition dahlias, which will grow higher, should be used in the rear border. Dahlias are prized for their cut flowers.

Dahlia hybrids

Height - 1 to 6 feet

Spread - 24 inches

Spacing - Plant in groups of two to three, 24 inches apart.

Exposure - full sun

Soil - Dahlia grows best in a well-drained soil that is slightly rich.

Bloom time - late July–first frost

Care - Dahlias are easy to maintain. They do not respond to soggy or wet soils. Pinch the shoot tips to promote fullness. It likes low-nitrogen fertilizer on a weekly basis. Water moderately and do not water late in the day.

Dahlia
Camano Choice

Gaillardia pulchella
Blanket flower

Description - A native plant of the western United States of America, this versatile annual is used for its ability to grow in all kinds of weather—drought or heat—and continue to flower. The very long blooming season is from June till frost. The flowers come in bright earth tone colors such as orange, rust, yellow, or gold. The shape and size of the flowers resemble daisies and are always neat and uniform. Blanket flower will mix very well with marigold and orange cosmos creating a fiery look. Many people mix them with shrubs and/or perennials in an informal border.

Height - 18 to 20

Spread - 15 inches

Spacing - Plant in groups of three to five, 15 inches apart.

Exposure - full sun

Soil - Blanket flower grows best in a well-drained soil that is not overly rich, but will grow in any garden soil. Important to note, it does not respond well to heavy clay soil.

Bloom time - mid-June–first frost

Care - Blanket flower are easy to maintain. They do not respond to soggy/wet soils. Pinch off faded flower heads to promote more blooms. Water moderately and do not water late in the day.

***Gaillardia pulchella* spp.**

Heliotropium arborescens
Heliotrope

Description - A native to Peru, this exotic plant is one of my favorite annuals. I love the variegated green and white leaves, which have an attractive white border with a green stripe. The bright purple flowers although small in size contrast well against the leaves. Each flower is about 1 inch in size, but the plant blooms in great profusion with flowers sitting atop the variegated stalks above the leaves. Heliotrope will grow in full sun or a light dappled shade but prefers sun. It is also highly valued for its vanillalike fragrance. An excellent cultivar is marine, which has deep blue flowers with a hint of purple. Use heliotrope as an edging plant, or mix it within the perennial border. Heliotrope is also great for containers. A classic combination is heliotrope with alyssum and ivy.

Height - 15 to 19 inches depending on the variety

Spread - 10 to 12 inches

Spacing - Plant in groups of three to five, 12 inches apart.

Exposure - sun or partial shade

Soil - Helitrope grows best in a well-drained soil that is slightly rich, but it will grow in any garden soil.

Bloom time - June—first frost

Heliotropium arborescens
Marine

Heliotropium arborescens
Marine

Care - Helitrope are easy to maintain. They do not respond to soggy or wet soils. Pinch off faded flower heads to promote more blooms. A heavy feeder, it needs regular fertilizing to promote vigorous growth. Water moderately and do not water late in the day.

Ipomoea
Morning Glory

Description - Native to the southeast United States, this climbing annual is probably the most popular climber and for good reason. It is grown both for its beautiful flowers and attractive foliage. In the same genus as moonflower vine, morning glory flowers open in the early morning and are spectacular. The flowers can be as large as 3 inches across and come in variety of blues, reds, and pinks. They bloom in great quantity from midsummer till frost. Use morning glory trained onto a trellis, fence, or other structure. It's also an excellent choice for containers as a cascading plant. A great use for morning glory is to mix it with moonflower vine for a very dramatic look.

Height - 12 feet

Spread - 30 inches

Spacing - plant as specimen

Exposure - full sun

Soil - Morning glory grows best in a well-drained soil that is of average fertility, but it will grow in any garden soil.

Bloom time - late June–first frost

Care - Morning glory are easy to maintain. They do not respond to soggy or wet soils. Water moderately and do not water late in the day.

Ipomoea **spp.**

Lobelia erinus
Edging Lobelia

Description - A native plant to South Africa, lobelia is a great plant for an annual ground cover, edging, or as a specimen in a rock garden. Its vivid blue, purple, or white flowers bloom in great quantity and cover the entire plant. Lobelia is a low grower that will spread up to 8 inches. It does not have a long bloom season (midspring to midsummer); for that reason, it should be mixed with other longer-blooming flowering annuals. Use lobelia in conjunction with marigolds for a great contrast.

Height - 8 inches

Spread - 8 inches

Spacing - Plant in groups of five to six, spacing 8 inches apart.

Exposure - full sun or partial shade

Soil - Lobelia grows best in a well-drained soil that is rich in organic matter but will grow in any garden soil.

Bloom time - late May–mid-August

Care - Lobelia are easy to maintain. They do not respond to soggy/wet soils. Cut back after first bloom to promote additional blooms. Water moderately and do not water late in the day.

Lobelia erinus spp.

Lobularia maritima
Sweet Alyssum

Description - A native plant to the Mediterranean region, sweet alyssum is a favorite for edging or as a specimen in a rock garden. Its small but plentiful flowers come in various shades of white, pink, red, or purple. Sweet alyssum has a long bloom season, from spring to the first frost. It is easy to care for as it tolerates poor soil quality and dry conditions. Sweet alyssum is a low grower that will spread up to 10 inches but is never invasive. It works well in the border front as a facer plant under taller species. Use sweet alyssum in conjunction with snapdragons and pinks (dianthus) for a great contrast.

Height - 4 inches

Spread - 8 inches

Spacing - Plant in groups of five to six, spacing 8 inches apart.

Exposure - full sun or partial shade

Soil - Sweet alyssum grows best in a well-drained soil that is rich in organic matter but will grow in any garden soil.

Bloom time - late April–mid-October

Care - Sweet alyssum are very easy to maintain. They do not respond to soggy or wet soils. Cut back after first bloom to promote additional blooms. Water moderately and do not water late in the day.

Lobularia Maritima

Mirabilis jalapa
Four o'clock

Description - This large annual is a native of South America. Four o'clock is a shrublike plant with beautiful flowers that opens in the late afternoon to evening. They are often situated near a deck or a patio so as the blooms open, it can be viewed while dining. Another interesting point is that, often, each plant will have different color flowers. Four o'clock flowers are available in yellow, white, red, pink, and a mixture of the above. Each bloom is about 2 inches in size and quite vivid in color. Use four o'clock in the perennial bed as a space filler or as a temporary shrub. A popular use is to line the driveway with four o'clock for a dramatic and colorful effect.

Height - 36 inches

Spread - 26 inches

Spacing - Plant in groups of two to three, spacing 24 inches apart.

Exposure - full sun or partial shade

Soil - Four o'clock grows best in a well-drained soil that is rich in organic matter, but it will grow in any garden soil.

Bloom time - late April–mid-August

Care - Four o'clock are easy to maintain. They do not respond to soggy or wet soils. Water moderately and do not water late in the day.

Mirabilis jalapa

Myosotis sylvatica
Forget-Me-Not

Description - A native plant to Asia, forget-me-not is a great plant for an annual ground cover, edging, or as a specimen in a rock garden. The bright blue flowers bloom in great quantity and cover the tops of each plant. Forget-me-not is a low grower that will spread up to 10 inches. It comes in many different varieties with some growing up to 15 inches tall, but the primary use is as an edging plant as it is a low grower. It does not have a long bloom season (from early spring to early summer), and it should be mixed with other longer blooming annuals. Forget-me-not will perform well in wet, boggy conditions and can be grown alongside a pond or stream. Use forget-me-not in conjunction with primrose and for a great contrast.

Height - 8 inches

Spread - 8 inches

Spacing - Plant in groups of five to six, spacing 8 inches apart.

Exposure - full sun or partial shade

Soil – Forget-me-not grows best in a well-drained soil that is rich in organic matter, but it will grow in any garden soil.

Bloom time - late March–mid-July

Care - Forget-me-not are easy to maintain. Water moderately and do not water late in the day.

Myosotis sylvatica
Victoria Blue

Ocimum basilicum
Basil

Description - A native plant to the tropics, basil is primarily grown as an herb, but it also has wonderful foliage and form that creates a dramatic effect. It is a great plant for a specimen in a rock garden or as a filler plant in a perennial bed. Basil's vivid foliage comes in a rich burgundy or a lush green color. Use basil in conjunction with dusty miller if using the burgundy foliage basil. The silver of dusty miller set against the burgundy of basil is outstanding.

If planting the green-color basil, mix it with the red-leaved begonia for a great contrast.

Height - 23 inches

Spread - 14 inches

Spacing - Plant in groups of one to two, spacing 12 inches apart.

Exposure - full sun

Soil - Basil grows best in a well-drained soil that is rich in organic matter.

Care - Basil are easy to maintain. They do not respond to soggy or wet soils. Water moderately and do not water late in the day.

Ocimum basilicum

Papaver
Annual Poppy

Description - Annual poppies are a nice addition to any garden. The flowers are very attractive and come in a wide variety of colors. Each flower is about 3 inches in size, cup shaped, and vividly colored. Poppy is used as a specimen plant in a rock garden or as part of an annual or perennial border. If there is any downside to poppies, it is that their bloom season is relatively short. Generally, they will bloom from midspring to early summer—around three to four weeks. Use annual poppies in conjunction with foxglove for a great look.

Height - 22 inches

Spread - 10 inches

Spacing - Plant in groups of three to four, spacing 10 inches apart.

Exposure - full sun

Soil - Poppy grows best in a well-drained soil that is rich in organic matter, but it will grow in any garden soil.

Bloom time - late May–mid-June

Care - Annual poppy are moderately easy to maintain. They require a little more feeding and certain insect species plague annual poppy more than the normal annual. They do not respond to soggy or wet soils. Water moderately and do not water late in the day.

Papaver
Rhoeas

Pelargonium × hortorum
Geranium

Description - This extremely popular plant is a native plant to South Africa. Geranium is popular for many reasons; it has beautiful flowers that bloom for a long period. The foliage is very attractive, and it is easy to care for. No wonder it is featured in nearly every garden in America. The foliage is attractive with its soft, variegated green and white colors. Geranium is a great potted plant; it will also work well in annual and perennial beds. Use geranium in conjunction with lobelia or other edging annuals for a great contrast.

Height - 20 inches

Spread - 17 inches

Spacing - Plant in groups of three to four, spacing 18 inches apart.

Exposure - full sun

Soil - Geranium grows best in a well-drained soil that is rich in organic matter.

Bloom time - late May– early October

Care - Geranium are easy to maintain. They do not respond to soggy/ wet soils. Pinch back or deadhead after the first bloom to promote additional blooms. Water moderately and do not water late in the day.

Pelargonium × Hortorum
William Languth

Salvia
Salvia

Description - Like its perennial relative, annual salvia is deer-proof and invaluable to the deer-proof garden. A native plant to the United States of America, salvia is a great plant for an annual flower bed, mixed in the perennial border, or as a specimen in a rock garden. It's vivid blue, purple, white, or red flowers bloom in great quantity and cover the entire plant top. Salvia has a long bloom season, especially so in the blue and red flower colors. Use salvia with virtually any other deer-proof annual for season-long color. I especially like red salvia mixed with marigolds for a fiery look.

Height - 20 inches

Spread - 12 inches

Spacing - Plant in groups of four to five, spacing 12 inches apart.

Exposure - full sun or light shade

Soil - Salvia grows best in a well-drained soil that is rich in organic matter, but it will grow in any garden soil.

Bloom time - late May–mid-October

Care - Salvia are very easy to maintain. They do not respond to soggy/wet soils. Deadhead after first bloom to promote additional blooms. Water moderately and do not water late in the day.

Salvia
Lady in Red

Senecio cineraria
Dusty Miller

Description - Perhaps the most popular of the annuals grown for their foliage, dusty miller is an invaluable addition to the deer-proof garden. A native plant to the Mediterranean region, dusty miller is an excellent plant for edging or mixed in the annual or perennial beds. The vivid silver/green foliage is delicate in appearance with finely cut leaves. Although dusty miller is primarily used for its foliage color and texture, it does flower. The flowers are yellow, offering a subtle contrast against the foliage. Each flower is about 1.5 inches in size, but they appear in great profusion during July, lasting a few weeks. Use dusty miller in conjunction with basil or wax begonia for a nice display.

Height - 12 inches

Spread - 10 inches

Spacing - Plant in groups of five to six, spacing 10 inches apart.

Exposure - full sun or partial shade

Soil - Dusty miller grows best in a well-drained soil that is rich in organic matter, but it will grow in any garden soil.

Care - Dusty miller are easy to maintain. They do not respond to soggy/wet soils. Water moderately and do not water late in the day.

***Senecio cineraria* spp.**

Tagetes
Marigold

Description - A native plant of Mexico, marigold is used virtually in every American garden and for good reason. Marigolds are great for edging along a walkway or mixed in the annual or perennial beds. Their vivid earth-tone flower colors such as orange, yellow, burgundy, and red are prized for their long blooming season and trouble-free blooms. I also like the shape and texture of marigold's foliage. Marigolds give off a strong scent and are often used in the vegetable garden to keep away insects and other pests. Use marigold in conjunction with blue- or white-flowering annuals to add a brilliant contrast.

Height - 15 inches

Spread - 12 inches

Spacing - Plant in groups of five to six, spacing 12 inches apart.

Exposure - full sun or partial shade

Soil - Marigold grows best in a well-drained soil that is rich in organic matter but will grow in any garden soil.

Bloom time - late May–end September

Care - Marigold are very easy to maintain. They do not respond to soggy/wet soils. Deadhead after first bloom to promote additional blooms. Water moderately and do not water late in the day.

Tagetes

Verbena × hybrida
Verbena

Description - A native plant to South America, verbena is prized for its ability to brighten up semishady spots. It is a nice plant for an annual ground cover, edging, or as a specimen in a rock garden. Its small but vivid-colored flowers come in a variety of colors from blue, purple, white, or red and bloom in great quantity. Verbena is a low grower that will spread up to 14 inches. It does not have a long bloom season (from early summer to early fall), and for that reason it should be mixed with other longer-blooming flowering annuals. Use verbena in conjunction with dahlia or marigolds for a great contrast.

Height - 10 inches

Spread - 12 inches

Spacing - Plant in groups of four to five, spacing 12 inches apart.

Exposure - full sun or partial shade

Soil - Verbena grows best in a well-drained soil that is rich in organic matter but will grow in any garden soil.

Bloom time - late June–end August

Care - Verbena are easy to maintain. They do not respond to soggy/wet soils. Water moderately and do not water late in the day.

***Verbena x hybrida* spp.**

Verbena x hybrida
Babylon Carpet Blue

Deer-Proof Vines

Vines are an important ingredient in most home gardens. They add height and dimension, hide and soften tall objects, and most have spectacular flowers. Vines can be grown on trellis, arbors, or on fences. They will add cooling shade to an overhead structure while allowing air to circulate. Vines are great for an overhead deck or patio to add screening and shade. Some gardeners grow vines up trees for an unusual look. Another popular use for vines is to grow them from containers. All in all, climbing vines can be a great addition to any home landscape. Fortunately, some of the very best species of vines are deer proof! As a side note, I personally do not favor growing vines directly onto your home. It presents too many maintenance problems for the homeowner. For example, some vines grow by means of suckers that are disc shaped. These suckers are almost impossible to remove once they attach themselves to a structure. When finally removed, they will leave a portion of itself on your walls, and the remainder will take the paint off the siding when pulled off! Other vines work their way inside or under bricks, tiles, and shingles. They will pull these objects away from the building while they continue to grow, creating a huge maintenance problem. In my opinion, it is simply not worth the risk, maintenance, cost, and repairs down the road to plant vines to grow on you're home.

Clematis
Clematis

Description - A native plant of Asia, clematis is a spectacular plant! It has beautiful flowers that bloom steadily during late spring and summer. Each flower is up to 6 inches across and almost star shaped. There is a wide choice of flower colors available—ranging from purple, blue, white, red, or pink—all quite beautiful. A two-color flower is available as well. One of the most popular clematis, the cultivar, the jackmani, with its deep purple flower color, is widely used. This long-living vine will gradually grow to up to 20 feet, depending on the species. Clematis is not invasive and easy to grow if you follow a few simple guidelines. This is a plant with a wide variety of species, some more shade tolerant than others. Clematis can also be container grown.

Zones - 6 to 9

Height - 18 to 20 feet

Spread - 4 feet

Spacing - Plant in groups of one to two, spacing 48 inches apart.

Exposure - full sun or partial shade

Soil - Clematis grows best in a well-drained soil that is rich in organic matter, but it will grow in any garden soil.

Bloom time - late June—end August

Care - Clematis are easy to maintain. They do not respond to soggy/wet soils. Mulch with compost, pine needles, or wood chips to keep clematis evenly moist. Fertilize every other week. Water moderately and do not water late in the day.

Clematis
Niobe

Clematis × jackmanii
Clematis spp.

Wisteria floribunda and sinensis
Wisteria

Description – A native plant of Eastern Asia, wisteria is probably the most popular of vines. Who can resist its abundance of weeping, lilac color, flowering racemes? There are two main cultivars of wisteria—floribunda and sinensis. The gardening purists will always choose sinensis, but they are interchangeable as far as I am concerned. The notable difference being floribunda's flowers are slightly larger in size than sinensis. All wisteria flowers are very attractive and scented. They bloom from the base upward at the same time as the leaves emerge creating a raceme. Each raceme is pendulous or weeping and about 12 inches long. The foliage is also attractive in its own right. Each leave is about 10 inches long and has up to nineteen leaflets. There is also a second blooming period during midsummer with smaller racemes. Wisteria can be trained to become treelike in appearance.

Wisteria Sinensis

Zones - five to ten

Height - 30 feet

Spread - 4 feet

Spacing - Plant in groups of one to two, spacing 48 inches apart.

Exposure - full sun

Soil - Wisteria grows best in a well-drained soil that is rich in organic matter.

Bloom time - late June and end August

Care - Wisteria are easy to maintain. They do not respond to soggy/wet soils. Mulch with compost, pine needles, or wood chips to keep wisteria evenly moist. Fertilize every other week. Prune each year. Water moderately and do not water late in the day.

Wisteria Sinensis

Deer-Proof Ground Covers

Ground covers are the backbone of every garden; they are virtually indispensable. Ground covers provide a base, a carpet if you will, in which to highlight other plants. They add form, texture, and dimension. They hide and soften bare areas. While some have attractive flowers, others have great-looking leaf shapes, textures and colors. Ground covers can be deciduous or evergreen. They are terrific performers for problem areas such as slopes or banks or those heavily shaded spots. Ground covers are also great for lining the base of a tree trunk to protect it from mower damage and to add a finished look to the lawn. Another common use is as an edging plant. Whatever your need for ground covers, you will find they never disappoint if given the slightest care and will be a steady performer year after year.

Fortunately, for those of us who have deer problems, there is a wide choice of popular ground covers not eaten by deer.

Aegopodium podagraria variegatum

Bishop's Weed - Varigated

Description - A deciduous perennial, bishop's weed is an attractive plant that is a vigorous grower. As it is deciduous, the foliage will die back in the fall and become renewed again in the spring. This is not the plant for the year-round carpeted effect. Bishop's weed foliage is very attractive with variegated green and white leaves. Each leaf is about 2 inches long and has a smartly striped white edge. The flowers are not spectacular in any way, small and barely noticeable sitting atop 3 feet stalks. It is the foliage that makes bishop's weed worthwhile, not the flowers. Bishop's weed will reseed itself by dropping seeds that will germinate in the spring. Bishop's weed grows in a spreading manner, much like a mat. All in all, a nice plant, but, because it is deciduous, I prefer other deer-proof ground covers.

To me, ground covers should keep its foliage year-round in order to be effective, but that is a personal choice.

Zones - 6 to 9

Height - 8 inches

Spread - 4 feet

Spacing - Plant in groups of five to six, spacing 36 inches apart.

Exposure - full sun or partial shade

Soil - Bishop's weed grows best in a well-drained soil that is rich in organic matter. It will also perform in poor garden soil.

Bloom time - late June

Care - Bishop's weed are easy to maintain. It does not respond well to soggy or wet soils. Water moderately and do not water late in the day. Mow each year to promote.

Aegopodium podagraria variegatum

Ajuga
Bugleweed/Carpet Bugle

Description - There are many species of ajuga. Some are suited more for rock gardens than as ground cover. The species I refer to for ground cover use is carpet bugle, which spreads by creeping runners. Carpet bugle is an attractive plant, grown for its foliage and handsome blue flowers. There are several cultivars available of carpet bugle, some with bronze leaves and others with dark purplish leaves. Overall, the foliage is very attractive with a leaf size between 2 to 4 inches and with a slight wave or curve to them. The leaves form a dense mat. In early spring, the flowers appear above the foliage. They are small but are a mid blue color that is striking. Unfortunately, the flowers do not last through the season; in fact, they appear for less than two weeks. Carpet bugle is an excellent ground cover for shade and semi-shade. It will grow in full sun but requires much more watering. A great use for carpet bugle is as a foundation plant or as edging along a shaded walkway.

Zones - 3 to 10

Height - 12 inches

Spread - ongoing

Spacing - Plant in groups of eight to ten, spacing 14 inches apart.

Exposure - full to partial shade

Soil - Ajuga grows best in a well-drained soil that is rich in organic matter. It will also perform in poor garden soil.

Bloom time - late June

Ajuga **spp.**

Ajuga
Atropurpurea

Care - Ajuga are easy to maintain. They do not respond to soggy/wet soils. Mow each year after bloom period to invigorate plants. Water moderately and do not water late in the day.

Convallaria
Lily of the Valley

Description - This widely used ground cover is one of the easiest ground covers to grow. Lily of the valley is noted for its swordlike foliage and its bell-shaped white flowers that give off a nice fragrance. Lily of the valley is deciduous, and, therefore, the foliage will die back in the fall and will be renewed in the spring. This is not the plant for the year-round carpeted effect. The plant spreads by underground stems called pips, which spread quite rapidly. Lily of the valley will grow in full shade but will have far less flowers than it would if planted in partial shade. The flowers are about one-fourth inch in size and appear in midspring, lasting until early summer. After flowering, small orange berries appear and last until the end of summer. Some uses for lily of the valley is in the rock garden, under trees or shrubs, or as edging. It is effective when mixed with ferns for a natural woodland look.

Zones - 3 to 9

Height - 3 to 8 inches

Spread - 14 inches

Spacing - Plant in groups of eight to ten, spacing 7 inches apart.

Exposure - full to partial shade

Soil - Lily of the valley grows best in a well-drained soil that is rich in organic matter. It will also perform in poor garden soil.

Bloom time - late June

Care - Lily of the valley are easy to maintain. It does not respond to soggy or wet soils. Water moderately and do not water late in the day.

***Convallaria majalis* spp**.

Epimedium
Barrenwort, Bishop's Hat

Description - This a plant that will grow and thrive even in the densest shade. Prized for its ability to fill barren areas and compete successfully with tree roots, barrenwort is an excellent ground cover for problem areas. It is easy to grow and relatively fast growing. In the northeast, barrenwort is semievergreen. Most of the foliage will die back after the first killing frost, but some will remain into late winter. In early spring, new growth emerges, which is a soft green color tinted with pink or rose color. The foliage then changes to a darker green in the summer, and by fall it turns to bronze. The flowers are attractive although small in size. They are similar to orchid in appearance, shaped much like a bishop's hat, and bloom in May. Barrenwort will grow well in the andromeda and mountain laurel bed as it prefers a slightly acidic soil.

Zones - 4 to 9

Height - 9 to 15 inches

Spread - ongoing

Spacing - Plant in groups of eight to ten, spacing 14 inches apart.

Exposure - Full to partial shade is best, but it will grow in full sun as well.

Soil - Barrenwort grows best in a well-drained soil that is rich in organic matter. It will also perform in poor garden soil, but it prefers a slightly acidic soil.

Bloom time -late May

Care - Barrenwort are easy to maintain. It does not respond to soggy/wet soils. Water moderately and do not water late in the day.

Epimedium versicolor
Sulphureaum

Lamium
Dead Nettle

Description - Dead nettle is one of my favorite ground covers for a number of reasons. First and foremost, it is extremely attractive. Its variegated foliage is noticeable from a distance; it brightens any shady spot. The flowers are quite nice, especially so for a ground-cover plant. It is also an easy plant to grow in any exposure, be it full sun or full shade. The foliage of dead nettle is small in size, only about one-half to 1 inch and has either white or yellow splashes of color. In the fall, the foliage turns to a pink or purple color that really stands out. The flowers are almost orchid shaped, very delicate, and bloom in the spring—almost always in a pink tone. They will bloom on and off until the summer. A widely used cultivar is beacon's silver, which has outstanding silvery green variegated leaves, mixed with bright pink flowers, providing a great contrast. Dead nettle is very easy to grow, spreads fast, and has no pest problems. It is not a commonly grown ground-cover plant when comparing it to pachysandra or ivy, but I feel it is far more interesting and attractive than either. Plant dead nettle in shady beds as an edging plant or mix it with ferns for a shade bed.

Zones – 5 to 10

Height - 6 to 9 inches

Spread - ongoing

Spacing - Plant in groups of eight to ten, spacing 10 inches apart.

Exposure - Full to partial shade is best, but it will grow in full sun as well.

Soil - Dead nettle grows best in a well-drained soil that is rich in organic matter. It will also perform in poor garden soil, but it prefers a slightly humus soil mixed in peat moss when planting.

Bloom time - late May

Care - Dead nettle are easy to maintain. They do not respond to soggy/wet soils. Water moderately and do not water late in the day.

Lamium
Beacon's silver

Lamium maculatum
Orchid Frost

Pachysandra
Japanese Spurge

Description - This plant is the most popular and widely used ground cover in the United States. The great popularity comes because it is a fast grower, grows in deep shade, and stays evergreen all year round. The foliage is a dark green color with leaves that are 2 to 4 inches long and wedge shaped. There is also a variegated variety available with green and white foliage. Pachysandra will grow in clusters and will create a dense carpet, staying consistently green throughout winter. The flowers are small and spike shaped. Always white, they are nowhere near spectacular, but the value of this plant is in its quick green-carpet effect, not the flowers. Pachysandra is always a reliable performer. It will thrive in full shade and is widely used as an understory plant for beds, under trees, and shrubs.

Zones - 5 to 10

Height - 6 to 12 inches

Spread - ongoing

Spacing - Plant in groups of eight to ten, spacing 8 inches apart.

Exposure - Full to partial shade is best. Do not plant in full sun.

Soil - Pachysandra grows best in a well-drained soil that is rich in organic matter. It will also perform in poor garden soil, but it prefers a slightly acidic soil.

Bloom time - late May

Care - Pachysandra are very easy to maintain. They do not respond to soggy or wet soils. Water moderately and do not water late in the day. Fertilize in early spring.

Pachysandra
Silver Edge

Pachysandra

Vinca minor
Periwinkle

Description - Vinca is another great ground-cover plant that thrives in shade. It has both pretty foliage and attractive flowers. A nice feature is that it grows rapidly while staying evergreen in the winter. The foliage is attractive in that each leaf is small, wedge shaped, and dark green with a glossy effect. There are also at least two variegated varieties available. Sterling silver has green and white foliage while the other variegated form, illumination, has green and yellow foliage. The most popular foliage choice is the solid green color however. In the spring, five-petaled bright blue flowers appear and bloom intermittently until fall. Vinca thrives in shade and will quickly establish itself in a shady bed. In full sun, the foliage may turn yellow, and the plant will not thrive. Keep vinca in part to full shade for the best performance. Vinca is a great ground cover for positioning under trees, in the shrub bed, or to stabilize a slope. It is easy to grow and has no serious pest problems

Zones - 4 to 9

Height - 4 to 6 inches

Spread - ongoing

Spacing - Plant in groups of eight to ten, spacing 12 inches apart.

Exposure - Full to partial shade is best.

Soil - Vinca grows best in a well-drained soil that is rich in organic matter. It will also perform in poor garden soil.

Bloom time - late April

Care - Vinca is easy to maintain. It does not respond to soggy/wet soils. Water moderately and do not water late in the day.

Vinca minor spp.

Vinca minor Spp.

Vinca minor
Sterling Silver

Deer-Proof Evergreen Shrubs and Trees

Evergreen shrubs and trees are the focal point of every garden. They are virtually indispensable. Evergreen shrubs and trees stabilize any landscape bed. They are there year after year, during the entire growing and non growing seasons. While other plants die back, leaving only the woody parts during the winter, evergreens become the focal point of the garden during the wintertime. The contrast of the dark green foliage of the evergreens set against the snow can be breathtaking to look at. Many evergreen shrubs produce terrific flowers and have interesting foliage. Some evergreen shrubs and trees are noted for their needles and pinecones; these are known as conifers. Finally, evergreens provide needed bird shelters for the resident winter birds. If you are encouraging birds to visit your yard, evergreen shrubs are vital as a feeding station in which birds can munch on their seed after visiting your feeder.

The evergreen shrub and tree category should be the starting point of any well landscaped home.

It should be noted, very few evergreen shrubs are totally deer proof. In fact, I can think of only *nine* species! After struggling with this decision, I have included evergreen shrubs that deer *may* occasionally eat a few leaves from. It is not common, and more often than not they will avoid these plants; but in the dead of winter, you may notice some missing shoots.

The plants that deer may occasionally eat will be marked with an * (asterisk) next to the plant's name. Finally, please note, I have grown all of the asterisked plants myself in my landscape or clients' landscapes with little or no damage from deer. This is the reason I decided to include these plants in this guide.

Berberis julianae
Wintergreen Barberry

Description - There are many
different species of barberry;
some are evergreen, and some are
deciduous. Certain cultivars are low
growers while others will grow 5 to 7
feet high and are suitable as hedges.
The two best cultivars from a
deer-proof standpoint are
wintergreen and Japanese barberry.
Wintergreen is a thorny plant that is
most effectively used for screening
or as a barrier. Its foliage is long and
slender shaped with spiny, toothed
edges. Each cluster of leaves has a
three-part thorny spine. The foliage
color in the growing season is dark

Berberis julianae spp.

green. In winter, the leaves change to a deep, rich burgundy color. Flowers are produced in April; they are
yellow, and although small and not spectacular, they are attractive. Small gray berries appear after the
flowering period.

Wintergreen barberry never needs pruning; it is a slow grower, and pruning removes its natural rounded form.
If left alone, it will grow to 6 to 8 feet in a dense, rounded form.
Wintergreen is easy to grow and has no serious pest problems.

Zones - 4 to 10

Height - 6 to 8 feet

Spread - 8 feet

Spacing - Plant in groups of three to four, spacing 4
feet apart for a hedge or as a single specimen plant.

Exposure - full sun to partial shade

Soil - Barberry grows best in a well-drained soil that
is rich in organic matter. Plant it in a protected spot
from drying winter winds.

Bloom time - late April

Care - Barberry is easy to maintain. Does not respond
to soggy/wet soils. Water moderately and do not
water late in the day.

Berberis julianae

Berberis julianae
Spring Flowers

Berberis thunbergii
Japanese Barberry

Description - Japanese barberry is widely used and easily recognized. It is a thorny plant that is most effectively used as a low-growing shrub either in a border or as a low-growing barrier. The best cultivar, in my opinion, is crimson pygmy. Crimson pygmy's foliage, as the name suggests, is a deep crimson color with spiny, toothed edges. It does have sharp pointed thorns, which can be painful to the touch. In winter, the leaves change to an even darker burgundy or crimson color. Flowers are produced in April. They are small and hardly noticeable.

Berberis thunbergii atropurpurea
Spring Flowers

Berries appear in the winter, adding some color. Another great cultivar with burgundy foliage is atropurpurea, which has slightly larger foliage and flowers than crimson pygmy. It also grows slightly larger. Japanese barberry never needs pruning; it is a slow grower, and pruning removes its natural rounded form. If left alone, it will grow to 3 to 4 feet in a dense, rounded form.

It is easy to grow and has no serious pest problems. There are many other varieties of Japanese barberry out there. Many have green foliage instead of the burgundy color I describe earlier. I have always felt the beauty of barberry is in the deep, rich burgundy color foliage that stays year round.

Berberis thunbergii
Crimson Pygmy

Japanese barberry is an excellent choice as a barrier hedge along a walkway or as a specimen in the rock garden.

Zones - 4 to 10

Height - 6 to 8 feet

Spread - 8 feet

Spacing - Plant in groups of three to four, spacing 4 feet apart for a low growing hedge, or as a grouping for a ground cover in the front of a bed or border

Exposure - full sun to partial shade

Soil - Japanese barberry grows best in a well-drained soil that is rich in organic matter. Plant it in a protected spot from drying winter winds.

Bloom time - late April

Berberis thunbergii atropurpurea
Fall Berries

Care - Japanese barberry is easy to maintain. It does not respond to soggy or wet soils. Water moderately and do not water late in the day.

Buxus sempervirens

Common or English Boxwood

Description - Used for centuries as a hedge or a specimen plant, boxwood is often thought of as the nucleus of a formal garden. It has few peers as an evergreen hedge as it responds well to pruning and stay inbounds. Boxwood can be pruned to virtually any shape. If left to its own devices, boxwood will slowly grow to 15 feet high and 20 feet wide. Boxwood stays dense from the ground up and slowly grows in a rounded form. Each leaf is small, dark green with a glossy effect. The flowers are quite small and inconspicuous, but boxwood is grown for its ability to stay in the same place for many years without overgrowing its location and not for its flowers. Boxwood is a slow grower but easy to grow and relatively pest free. It is an excellent choice as a foundation plant or as hedge along a walkway.

Zones - 5 to 10

Height - 10 to 15 feet (unpruned)

Spread - 15 feet (unpruned)

Spacing - Plant in groups of five to six, spacing 4 to 5 feet apart for a hedge or as a single specimen. plant

Exposure - full sun to partial shade

Soil - Boxwood grows best in a well-drained soil that is rich in organic matter. Plant it in a protected spot from drying winter winds.

Bloom time - late April

Buxus sempervirens

Buxus sempervirens

Care - Boxwood is fairly easy to maintain. It does not respond to soggy/wet soils. Each year, prune out the inner dead wood and remove any fallen leaves caught inside the plant. This will help to prevent twig canker disease. Boxwood does not tolerate drought conditions. On extremely high-temperature days, be sure to water in thoroughly. Water moderately and do not water late in the day.

Cotoneaster
Cotoneaster

Description - There are many species of cotoneaster. Most are used as a low-growing and spreading shrub. Certain cultivars make excellent ground cover for small areas. I have had no incidents of heavy feeding on my cotoneaster, and for this reason, I feel comfortable recommending it as a reasonable risk. Cotoneaster is a great low-growing shrub used as filler for barren areas. One species, dammeri, is evergreen in my home zone of 5A while many others are either semi evergreen or deciduous. All produce small red berries that contrast well with the glossy dark green foliage. In the spring, small white flowers are borne atop the foliage, creating a very nice contrast. Cotoneaster will grow both in full sun and in partial shade. They prefer slightly acidic soil, making cotoneaster perfect for planting with andromeda, leucothoe, mountain laurel, and other acid-loving plants. Use cotoneaster in the rock garden as a slope stabilizer or as ground cover under shrubs. Another great use for cotoneaster is as a draping plant over a stonewall.

Cotoneaster horizontallis
Spring Flowers

Cotoneaster
Affinis

Cotoneaster horizontalis
Fall In Full Fruit

Zones - 5 to 10

Height - 1 to 3 feet

Spread - ongoing

Spacing - Plant in groups of three to four, spacing 2 feet apart.

Exposure - full sun to partial shade

Soil - Cotoneaster grows best in a well-drained soil that is slightly rich in organic matter and slightly acidic. It will not tolerate heavy clay-type soil or overly wet soils.

Bloom time - late May

Cotoneaster horizontalis
Fall In Full Fruit

Care - Cotoneaster is fairly easy to maintain. It does not respond to soggy or wet soils. Cotoneaster is susceptible to fire blight, mites, and leaftier. Water moderately and do not water late in the day.

Hollies

There are literally hundreds of holly species. Some species are evergreen, and some are deciduous. Hollies are valued for their interesting toothed or spined foliage, their colorful berries, their shape, and their form. Only two holly species that I know of are deer resistant. In fact, only the holly opaca is totally deer proof. The other species, like Chinese holly, is deer resistant but could potentially lose some growth from browsing in high-risk areas and during the high-risk time of the year.

Ilex cornuta
Ospring

Ilex cornuta
Chinese Holly

Description - Chinese holly is a classic holly in the sense that when one thinks of holly, the form and shape of Chinese holly comes to mind. There are many different cultivars of Chinese holly. Some cultivars grow in a rounded form with a spread and height of 3 to 5 feet. These varieties are excellent as foundation plantings. Other cultivars grow to 10 feet and will form a pyramidal shape. These varieties are excellent for mass plantings or as screens. All Chinese holly are notable for the ability of the female plants to produce berries without a male counterpart nearby to pollinate it.

Ilex cornuta burfordi
Fall Berries

The foliage is a very attractive, dark green with five spines or teeth. One variety, named ospring, has beautiful variegated green and yellow leaves. Another great variety is rotunda, which grows in a mounding, low-growing globe effect. Depending on the species, the leaves will be from 2 to 4 inches in size. The flowers are barely noticeable, but hollies are not grown for their flowers but for their form, foliage, and berries. The fruit or berries are produced in the fall and are about one-fourth inch in size with a vibrant red color. They make a beautiful contrast to the glossy dark green foliage.

Zones - 6 to 10

Height - 3 to 11 feet (depending on the variety)

Spread - up to 15 feet (depending on the variety)
Exposure - full sun to partial shade

Ilex cornuta
Rotunda

Soil - Hollies grow best in a well-drained soil that is rich in organic matter. All species prefer a slightly acidic soil. Plant it in a protected spot from drying winter winds.

Bloom time - flowers in April, produces fruit in fall

Care - Some care is needed to keep plants healthy. Hollies are susceptible to a number of serious pests such as leaf miners and scale. They do not respond to soggy or wet soils. Water moderately and do not water late in the day.

Ilex cornuta burfordi
Fall Berries

Ilex opaca
American Holly

Description - From a deer-proof standpoint, American holly will outperform the Chinese holly. If you are looking for the one holly that will not suffer any deer damage at all, go with American holly. They are not considered the finest form of holly, but the major value to those of us with heavy deer population is they will not suffer damage. All in all, American holly is an attractive plant that looks like what a holly should look like. There are many species available today. Many cultivars are grown locally and will be better for the Boston garden than, say, the Bedford, New York garden. Consult with your local nursery to determine where the plants were grown. If they are grown in your local area, it is always preferable. American hollies can reach a height of 30 feet. Its basic form is pyramidal with branches that are dense with foliage. Not known as a fast grower, it will slowly reach its maximum height potential. The foliage is between 2 to 4 inches depending on the species. Most have many spiny teeth along the edges and are a dark glossy green. The flowers are barely noticeable, but hollies are not grown for their flowers but for their form, foliage, and berries. The fruit or berries are produced in the fall and are about one-fourth inch in size with a vibrant red color. They make a beautiful contrast to the glossy dark green foliage.

Ilex opaca howard
Fall Berries

Zones - 6 to 9

Height - 12 to 32 feet (depending on the variety)

Spread - up to 15 feet (depending on the variety)

Exposure - full sun to partial shade

Soil - Hollies grow best in a well-drained soil that is rich in organic matter. All species prefer a slightly acidic soil. Plant it in a protected spot from drying winter winds.

Bloom time - flowers in April, produces fruit in fall

Care - Some care needed to keep plants healthy. Hollies are

Ilex opaca
Miss Helen

Ilex opaca
Mary Holman

susceptible to a number of serious pests such as leaf miners and scale. They do not respond to soggy or wet soils. Water moderately and do not water late in the day.

Juniperus chinensis
Chinese Juniper

Description - The juniper family consists of about seventy species, many of which are not deer proof. I have found the only reliable juniper species that is deer proof is the Chinese juniper. Fortunately, Chinese juniper has many different cultivars from ground covers to upright forms that can reach 30 feet in their lifetime. Foliage colors vary from golden yellow, to dark green, to a bluish green. Chinese junipers are noted for their versatility, toughness, and dependability. They will grow in virtually any soil and prized for their ability to be long lived. All Chinese junipers have needlelike foliage and will produce cones that are a blue/green color. The cones actually resemble berries more so than cones and are about a one-half inch in size. As there are so many varieties of Chinese juniper, I will list only the very best and most popular cultivars.

Juniperus chinensis

San Jose is a low-growing form used as a ground cover. It will grow up to 6 feet wide with a height of 1.5 feet. The foliage color is a soft green and is made of needlelike leaves. Excellent for stabilizing slopes.

Sargenti is another excellent ground cover choice with blue/green color foliage and soft needles. Sargenti will spread up to 9 feet with a height of 1.5 feet.

Gold coast is known for its golden yellow foliage. It will gradually grow to a height and spread of 4 to 6 feet.

Hetzii is an upright form that will reach up to 17 feet. The blue/green foliage color and bluish cones are outstanding features.

There are many other species of Chinese junipers, but the above varieties are some of the most popular. In many parts of the country, junipers are grown locally. Check with your nursery to find the form that is grown in your area for best results.

Zones - 4 to 10

Height - 1 to 20 feet (depending on the variety)

Spread - up to 15 feet (depending on the variety)

Exposure - full sun

Soil - Junipers grow best in a well-drained soil.

Japanese chinensis
Gold coast

Juniperus chinensis
Hetzii

Juniperus chinensis
Sargenti

Care - Junipers are fairly easy to grow. They are susceptible to a few serious pests such as bagworms and mites. Both can be controlled by insecticide. They do not respond to soggy or wet soils. Water moderately and do not water late in the day.

Kalmia latifolia
Mountain Laurel

Description - As noted by the asterisk, mountain laurel may occasionally suffer from deer browsing. Personally, I have used mountain laurel for years in my own garden and in other gardens and have found little damage from deer. Occasionally, there may be a few shoots missing on younger plants, but overall I consider it a reasonable risk as I consider mountain laurel a truly spectacular landscape plant. Mountain laurel is a native plant that grows along the east coast. In its best form, mountain laurel will grow to an almost-treelike shrub. It will stay dense if planted in the right location, which is partial shade. In full sun, it will grow leggy with little undergrowth. It is far better suited when positioned in partial shade. Mountain laurel has a truly beautiful flower; in fact, it is the state flower of both Connecticut and Pennsylvania. Each flower is small

Kalmia latifolia
Freckles

individually but blooms in large clusters in late May and June. The buds are a rich pink color before opening; when opened, the flowers become a pale pink color. The foliage color is a dark glossy green color that contrasts well with the flowers. When the foliage is new, it emerges as a light yellowish to green color and gradually turns to dark green. Each leave may be up to 4 to 5 inches long and is sword like in its shape. Overall, mountain laurel is a great plant that should be used in every garden. It is not overly difficult to grow and does not suffer from any serious pest problems. It occasionally suffers from leaf spot mildew, which can be remedied by spraying. A few terrific cultivars are freckles with pink flowers and burgundy contrasting borders. Another showy cultivar is raspberry glow, which has red buds that open to pink blooms. The contrast between the bud color and the flower color is spectacular.

Mountain laurel is best used as a foundation plant to soften corners or as a woodland plant along a rustic path. It mixes very well with other acid-loving plants such as cotoneaster, andromeda, leucothoe, and hollies. In that setting, mountain laurel will perform well.

Zones - 3 to 9

Height - 6 to 15 feet

Spread - up to 15 feet

Exposure - partial shade

Soil - Mountain laurel grows best in a well-drained soil that is rich in organic matter and acidic. It prefers the soil to be slightly moist but *never* constantly wet and heavy. In those conditions, mountain laurel will fail. Plant it in a protected spot from drying winter winds.

Bloom time - flowers in late May/early June

Care - Mountain laurel is fairly easy to grow. It does not respond to soggy or wet soils. Certain insect species may cause minor problem, but spraying can remedy this. Water moderately and do not water late in the day. My plants experience leaf spot, which can be remedied by a regular spray program.

Kalmia Latifolia spp.

Kalmia Latifolia spp.

Kalmia Latifolia spp.

Kalmia latifolia
Raspberry Glow

Leucothoe fountanesiana
Drooping Leucothoe

Description - Leucothoe is a great low-growing plant that mixes very well with mountain laurel, andromeda, and other acid-loving plants. Native to the Appalachian Mountain area, leucothoe prefers shady woodland settings, where it can spread. Leucothoe is noted for its foliage color that will change as the seasons progress. The foliage emerges as either bright green or bronze (depending on the cultivar) and will gradually turn to a purplish color in winter. Some varieties such as rainbow are variegated with a blend of yellow, green, and pink foliage. This plant is truly spectacular and changes as the season progresses. Another terrific variegated cultivar is catesbaei. The leaf colors of catesbaei are a blend of green and ivory while the older leaves turn purple, producing a great contrast.

Leucothoe fountanesiana
Rainbow

All leucothoe leaves will grow up to 7 inches long, are sword shaped, and are handsome.

Leucothoe grows in an arching form and remains a somewhat low-growing shrub.

The flowers are white, slightly fragrant, and small individually. They hang in racemes below the leaves, almost hidden from view, but are very attractive.

Leucothoe is not to be planted as a featured flowering shrub. It is used more for its growth form, its foliage shape, and its color. I find the best use for leucothoe is positioned in a woodland setting as a low-growing mass of shrubs. Another good use for leucothoe is as a facer plant, positioned under leggy shrubs (mountain laurel and older andromeda can become quite leggy). Leucothoe will also perform well as a slope stabilizer.

Zones - 6 to 10

Height - 2 to 5 feet (depending on the variety)

Spread - up to 6 feet (depending on the variety)

Exposure - partial shade to shade

Soil - Leucothoe grows best in a well-drained soil that is rich in organic matter. All species prefer a slightly acidic soil. Plant it in a protected spot from drying winter winds.

Bloom time - flowers in April

Care - Leucothoe is easy to grow if planted in the right location. It does not respond to sunny locations or dry soil. It needs to be positioned in a setting that is similar to its native setting. Slightly wet, acidic soil is best. Leucothoe never needs pruning as this will ruin its natural shape. It does not respond to soggy or wet soils. Water moderately and do not water late in the day.

Leucothoe fountanesiana
Catesbaei

Leucothoe fountanesiana spp.

Leucothoe fountanesiana s

Leucothoe fountanesiana s
Fall Color

Picea abies
Norway Spruce

Description - Related to blue spruce, the Norway spruce is slightly less deer resistant than blue spruce. Don't let this stop you from planting Norway spruce. My experience is that deer seldom browse on Norway spruce, and when they do, they do not consume much material. They may grab a few shoots here or there, but it is not common. For the large-scale landscape, Norway spruce is unsurpassed. Use it as a specimen plant for the eye to focus on from a distance or as a mass planting for a screen or a windbreak. Some dwarf varieties are very low growing and work well in the small specimen garden as an evergreen accent.

Norway spruce seems to get better with age. In its youth, it grows upright and almost stiff. As it ages, it opens and becomes more graceful with slightly weeping branches. The tree form will grow to 90 feet high with a spread of 35 feet, so plant accordingly.

Some of the best cultivars are remonti for a conical-shaped tree reaching about 30 feet.
Nidiformis (bird's nest spruce) is a great low-growing and spreading variety that can be used instead of juniper as an evergreen and needled specimen plant. It also blends very well with mugho pine and juniper. For a weeping variety, pendula is an excellent choice.

Zones - 2 to 9

Height – 3 to 90 feet (depending on the variety)

Spread - up to 40 feet (depending on the variety)

Exposure - Full sun is for best color. Partial shade is OK.

Soil - Norway spruce grows best in a well-drained soil that is rich in organic matter. Plant it in a protected spot from drying winter winds.

Bloom time - Cones are produced in fall.

Care - Norway spruce is easy to grow if planted in the right location. It does not respond to shady locations or overly dry soil. They do not perform well in soggy or wet soils, either. Water moderately and do not water late in the day.

***Picea abies* spp.**
New Spring Growth

Picea abies
Nidiformis

Picea Abies Remonti

Picea abies pendula

*Picea glauca
White Spruce

Description - Related to both blue spruce and Norway spruce, the white spruce is slightly less deer resistant than blue spruce. However, some varieties such as Alberta (a.k.a. conica) are totally deer proof. From this genus, I recommend only the Alberta Spruce. Another good reason for selecting only Alberta spruce is that the larger white spruce cultivar is not as striking as its relative, the Norway spruce.

In a formal landscape bed, dwarf Alberta spruce is a must. Use it as a singular specimen plant mixed with other evergreen shrubs. Alberta grows quite slowly and stays in a pyramid form. After twenty-five years, its height will be no more than 9 to 10 feet. It is also excellent as a front-door shrub or as driveway-entrance shrub.

Zones - 1to 9

Height - 3 to 60 feet (depending on the variety)

Spread - up to 20 feet (depending on the variety)

Exposure - Full sun is for best color. Partial shade is OK.

Soil - Alberta spruce grows best in a well-drained soil that is rich in organic matter. Plant it in a protected spot from drying winter winds.

Bloom time - Cones are produced in fall.

Care - Alberta spruce is easy to grow if planted in the right location. It does not respond to shady locations or overly dry soil, but be sure the soil is not overly soggy. Water moderately and do not water late in the day.

Picea glauca
Rainbows End
New Spring Growth

Picea glauca
Alberta Spruce

Picea pungens
Colorado Blue Spruce

Description - There are several varieties of blue spruce, from a treelike shape and form to a shrublike low-growing plant. Fortunately, blue spruce species are completely deer proof. They truly belong in every garden as they are an outstanding landscape plant. All blue spruce have short sharp needles that are a distinctive blue green color. Each needle is about three quarter inch long. The needle color is truly unique and contrasts well in any setting. Blue spruce needs full sun for best color, but it will grow in partial shade as well. The cones are hanging and egg shaped.

Picea pungens

Most blue spruce cultivars grow in a pyramidal shape and are dense from the ground up. Some of the more noted varieties are glauca, which is quite blue and dense in form. Hoopsi is a low-growing and compact variety—almost shrub like in form. It makes for a great specimen plant. Glauca pendula is a weeping form, also great as a specimen.

Zones - 2 to10

Height - 10 to 50 feet (depending on the variety)

Spread - up to 8 feet (depending on the variety)

Exposure - Full is sun for best color. Partial shade is OK.

Soil - Colorado blue spruce grows best in a well-drained soil that is rich in organic matter. Plant it in a protected spot from drying winter winds.

Bloom time - Cones are produced in fall.

Care - Colorado blue spruce is easy to grow if planted in the right location. It does not respond to shady locations or overly dry soil but will not tolerate an overly soggy soil either. Water moderately and do not water late in the day.

Picea pungens
Glauca globosa

Picea pungens
Glauca pendula

Pieris japonica
Andromeda, Lily of the Valley Shrub

Description - This group of evergreen plants are my absolute favorite shrubs and for good reason. Andromeda is the deer-proof gardener's delight! They are 100 percent deer proof; in fact, deer avoid andromeda like the plague because its foliage is poisonous. Andromeda are easy to grow and beautiful year-round. This species should be your starting point for flowering deer-proof shrubs, period! There are several species of andromeda, all have clusters of small bell-shaped flowers very similar to lily of the valley flowers. In most species, the flower color is white, but in recent cultivars, pink is the flower color. All andromeda grow

Pieris japonica
Dorothy Wycoff

in a compact and neat form until it gradually reaches a height of 6 to 12 feet. The foliage is highly attractive in its own right. Some cultivars such as forest flame and mountain fire have spectacular, fiery red foliage as new growth. They are very showy and beautiful. Andromedas flower in early spring and are a welcome sight to a gardener's eye after a long winter. Cultivar Dorothy Wycoff's foliage will have tints of burgundy mixed with green leaves in winter along with pink flowers in the early spring.

It should be noted, some cultivars are susceptible to lace bug, which can be a serious pest for this plant. Do not plant andromeda in full sun, which lace bugs favor. I find the lace bug condition to be less prevalent in shaded areas, which Andromeda actually prefer. There is one cultivar, however, pieris floribunda that has no problems with lace bugs, whatsoever.

Zones – 4 to10

Height- 3 to 12 feet (depending on the variety)

Spread - up to 9 feet (depending on the variety)

Exposure - partial to full shade

Soil - Andromeda grows best in a well-drained soil that is rich in organic matter and slightly acidic. Plant it in a protected spot from drying winter winds.

Bloom time - March/early April

Pieris japonica
Mountain Fire

Pieris japonica
Amamiana

Pieris spp.
Spring Flowers

Pieris spp.
Summer

Care - Andromeda is easy to grow if planted in the right location. Andromeda does not respond well to sunny locations. They do not respond to soggy or wet soils either. Lace bug is a serious pest, but it can be controlled by spraying. Leaf spot is another problem; this fungus can also be controlled by spraying.

Pinus mugo
Mugho Pine

Description - This group of needled evergreen plants are widely used as a specimen in a formal bed or as a foundation plant. It is prized for its low-growing form and shape and its foliage. The growth form of mugho pine is a rounded and mounding shape; in its youth, it will remind some of a pincushion. Foliage is a deep, dark green color with needles ranging from 1 to 3 inches in length. New growth or candles sprout in spring with a lime green color, giving the foliage a subtle and pleasing contrast. Although a very slow grower, some cultivars eventually reach a height of 6 to 15 feet, depending on the variety. There are several lower-growing varieties available, and this is the most common use for mugho pine. It excels as a low-growing specimen, staying low with a manageable spread. The best low-growing cultivars are compacta or gnome, which will grow up to 4 feet tall. To keep mugho pine compact, each "candle" or new growth can be pruned back up to three-fourth of the length of the candle. I use mugho pine in a variety of beds and landscape areas without any deer damage, and I encourage you to do the same. It is easy to grow and suffers from no serious pest problems. Some of the best uses for mugho pine are in the rock garden or in a formal specimen bed. It mixes very well with other conifers, such as Alberta spruce, conica, and Norway spruce nidiformis, lending itself to an Oriental-style evergreen bed. The different textures, shapes, and shades of green create a beautiful, formal garden bed.

Zones - 2 to 9

Height - 3 to 15 feet (depending on the variety)

Spread - up to 4 to 9 feet (depending on the variety)

Exposure - full sun to partial shade

Soil - Mugho pine grows best in a well-drained soil that is rich in organic matter and slightly acidic. Plant it in a protected spot from drying winter winds.

Bloom time - Cones are produced in fall.

Care - Mugho pine is easy to grow if planted in the right location. They do not respond to soggy/wet soils. Scale can be a slight problem but is easily controlled. Water moderately and do not water late in the day.

Pinus mugo
Compacta

Pinus nigra
Austrian Pine

Description - This group of needled evergreen plants are widely used as a lawn specimen plant or as a windbreak or screen. Austrian pine is an interesting tree because of its growth shape and form. In its youth, Austrian pine grows in a pyramidal form. As it ages, it becomes more open and irregular in its shape. Eventually, it will grow to a height of 60 feet with a spread of 25 feet. Austrian pine barks develop a different mottling of colors that stand out in the winter landscape. Its foliage is dark green and stiff needles that are up to 4 inches long. The Austrian pine can be plagued by several fungus problems, and it eventually can be killed from these threats. Although Austrian pine is a nice-looking plant, I prefer *Pinus strobus* (white pine) because it is similar in look to Austrian pine, but it has none of the pest/fungus problems that plague Austrian pine.

Zones - 4 to 9

Height - 35 to 60 feet
(depending on the variety)

Spread - up to 25 feet
(depending on the variety)

Exposure - full sun to
partial shade

Soil - Austrian pine grows best
in a well-drained soil that is rich
in organic matter and slightly
acidic. Plant it in a protected
spot from drying winter winds.

Bloom time - Cones are
produced in fall.

Care - Austrian pine is easy to
grow. They do not respond
to soggy/wet soils. Water
moderately and do not water
late in the day.

Pinus nigra

Pinus strobus
White Pine

Description - White pine is one of
the fastest-growing pine species. If
you are looking for a quick screen
or windbreak, white pine is perfectly
suited for that purpose. It is also widely
used as a lawn specimen plant. White
pine will grow in a pyramidal form
in youth; it will eventually grow to
become more open and graceful as it
ages. Its branches will also grow out
horizontally as it grows older. Foliage
is handsome with each needle up to
5 inches long and a rich blue, green
color. The cones of the white pine are
very attractive; they can be up to 6
inches long and irregular shaped. White
pine is very effectively used as a hedge;
up to three-fourth of its new growth
(candles) can be controlled by pruning.
Although deer may occasionally grab a

Pinus stobus spp.

shoot or two of its new growth, I find white pine to be a dependable performer with little or no deer damage.

Zones - 3 to 9

Height - 35 to 100 feet (depending on
the variety)

Spread - up to 40 feet (depending on the variety)

Exposure - full sun to partial shade

Soil - White pine grows best in a well-drained soil that is rich in
organic matter and slightly acidic. Plant it in a protected spot
from drying winter winds.

Bloom time - Cones are produced in fall.

Care - White pine is easy to grow if planted in the right location.
They do not respond to soggy/wet soils. Spittlebug can be a
slight problem but is easily controlled by spraying. Generally, the
first application will solve the problem.

***Pinus strobus* spp.**

Pinus sylvestris
Scotch Pine

Description - Scotch pine is widely used as a Christmas tree for both live and cut trees. Beyond that use, it is a great landscape plant. What makes Scotch pine unusual is its bluish color needles, which contrasts well with its relative, the white pine. Each needle is up to 4 inches long and can last up to four years. Another unusual feature of Scotch pine is its bark, which is highly textured and red/brown in color. The bark peels off in papery flakes, giving it an ancient look. Scotch pine is one of the few pines that will tolerate shearing, for that reason it makes a great hedge. It is also highly resistant to wind; a popular use is as a windscreen. Scotch pine will grow in a pyramidal form in youth and gradually become more open and graceful with age. It will ultimately reach a height of 25 feet. Some of the best varieties are watereri, which grows in a dense pyramidal form and has rich blue needles. Fastigiata is another great cultivar growing more in a columnar form and having blue/green needles.

Use Scotch pine as a specimen tree or as a screen.

Zones - 4 to 9

Height - 15 to 25 feet (depending on the variety)

Spread - up to 15 feet (depending on the variety)

Exposure - full sun to light shade

Soil - Scotch pine grows best in a well-drained soil that is rich in organic matter and slightly acidic.

Bloom time - Cones are produced in fall.

Care - Scotch pine is easy to grow if planted in the right location. It does not respond to soggy or wet soils. Spittlebug can be a slight problem but is easily controlled by spraying. Water moderately and do not water late in the day.

***Pinus sylvestris* spp.**
Interesting Bark

Pinus sylvestris
Watereri

Deer-Proof Deciduous Shrubs and Trees

By definition, deciduous shrubs will lose their leaves in the fall and will grow new leaves in the spring. Deciduous shrubs and trees are sometimes called the stars of the spring-to-fall landscape. In spring, their flowers are quite beautiful; during summer, their foliage can offer cooling shade and a colorful contrast; and finally, during the fall the foliage can be truly spectacular. Even in the dead of winter without foliage, deciduous shrubs and trees can be interesting because of their bark or form against the winter skylight. Deciduous shrubs and trees are a valuable addition to any landscape and should be an important part of yours.

Please note, many deciduous shrubs and trees are not totally deer proof. Some species are left completely alone by deer during spring and summer but are very lightly browsed during the late-fall season. My feeling on this is that since the plant is about to lose its leaves anyway, it is not a big deal if a few shoots or leaves are lost to deer browsing. Once the plants lose all the leaves during late fall, the deer will leave the plant alone during winter. Based on this reasoning, I have included deciduous shrubs and trees that deer *may* occasionally eat a few shoots of. It is not common, and more often than not, they will avoid these plants; however, I want you to be aware of this.

The plants that deer may occasionally eat will be marked with an * (asterisk) next to the plant name.

Finally, please note, I have grown all of the asterisked plants myself in my landscape or clients' landscapes with little or no damage from deer. This is the primary reason that I decided to include these plants in this guide.

Betula papyrifera
Paper Birch

Description - There are approximately forty different species of birches. One of the most popular species is paper birch. It is sometimes called canoe birch because its bark is waterproof; the paper birch was widely used for making canoes by Native Americans. The beauty of paper birch is indeed in its silvery white-colored bark that stands out in any setting. The bark, with time, will peel in paper like layers. Another bonus is its foliage, which is a nicely rounded shape with serrated edges and an attractive green color in season. During fall, the leaves change to a brilliant yellow. The flowers are inconspicuous and become hanging catlins during the season, which are attractive although small.

Paper birch is best used as a lawn highlight, where the bark color can be highlighted against the green of the lawn.

Zones - 2 to 9

Height - 50 to 75 feet

Spread - up to 45 feet

Exposure - full sun to light shade

Soil - Birch grows best in a well-drained soil that is rich in organic matter and slightly acidic.

***Betula papyrifera* spp**
Summer

Care - Birch is easy to grow if planted in the right location. Birch borer and birch miner can be a slight problem, but they are easily controlled with regular spraying. Water moderately and do not water late in the day.

***Betula papyrifera* spp.**
Summer

***Betula papyrifera* spp.**
Fall Color

***Betula papyrifera* spp.**

Betula pendula
European White Birch

Description - Closely related to paper birch, European white birch shares many of the same characteristics as paper birch. It is slightly less deer resistant than paper birch, but browsing will not be a major problem. The bark of white birch is a silvery white color that has splashes of black. Like paper birch, white birch foliage is nicely rounded in shape with serrated edges and a dark green color in season. During fall, the leaves change to a brilliant yellow. The flowers are inconspicuous and become hanging catlins during the season, which are attractive however small. White birch is a faster grower than paper birch and is better suited for screening when planted in groves. The effect of several white birches planted in groves can be breathtaking against the winter skyline. There are several different cultivars available in white birch. Some grow in a columnar form while others are cultivated to become weeping in form. Youngii is an excellent weeping form and the most widely used for that purpose. White birch is an excellent choice as a lawn specimen tree, where the bark color can be highlighted against the green of the lawn. Especially dramatic for that use is the weeping version.

Zones - 2 to 9

Height - 25 to 35 feet

Spread - up to 15 feet

Exposure - full sun to light shade

Soil - Birch grows best in a well-drained soil that is rich in organic matter and slightly acidic.

Care - Birch are easy to grow if planted in the right location. Birch borer and birch miner can be slight problems but are easily controlled with regular spraying. Water moderately and do not water late in the day.

Betula Pendula
Youngii

Betula pendula spp.

Betula pendula spp.
Fall color

Betula pendula spp.
Summer

Cornus florida
Flowering Dogwood

Description - Flowering dogwoods are extremely popular trees in the northeast garden. Native to the east coast, those of us lucky enough to be living here will achieve success growing dogwoods as they do not grow well out of their native area. Flowering dogwoods are known for their pyramidal form in growth and their four-season beauty—spectacular spring flowers, lovely summer foliage with fruits appearing later in the season, and then a blaze of orange and burgundy leaves. Flowering dogwood bark is also a feature as it is distinctive on its own merits. Dogwood flowers are large and beautiful with four bract petals forming a star in shape. The flowers are depending on the species—pink, red, or white. Pink is the most widely used however. A dogwood in full bloom can be quite an impressive sight!

Cornus florida
F. Ruba

The foliage is also attractive with a heart-shaped leaf and a nice medium green color. Fruit appears toward fall; a vivid red berry set against green leaves, it is spectacular to look at. Then, the fall show begins with brilliant orange and burgundy leaves, a truly magnificent sight. Dogwood will slowly grow to a manageable height and spread. They are perfect for a specimen lawn tree or as a foundation plant to soften a corner.

Unfortunately, I must tell you, there is a major problem with flowering dogwoods; it is a recent disease called anthraconose fungus or lower dieback disease. It has really wrecked havoc on this tree, and flowering dogwood should be used with caution. Trees that are planted in a shady location are more prone to this disease than the trees planted in open sunny locations. Another possible cause is lawn mower damage to the trunk. It can be controlled by spraying if not too far gone, but it's far better to plant flowering dogwood in the best setting for it to thrive.

It is interesting to note that *Cornus kousa* (Korean dogwood) is free from this disease, but in my opinion from an aesthetic standpoint, flowering dogwood is the superior species.

Zones - 5 to 9

Height - 12 to 16 feet

Spread - up to 12 feet

Exposure - full sun to light shade

Soil - Flowering dogwood grows best in a well drained soil that is rich in organic matter and slightly acidic.

Bloom time - May

Care - Flowering dogwood can be difficult to grow if planted in the wrong location. Anthraconose fungus, or lower dieback disease has become a major problem recently. Water moderately and do not water late in the day.

Cornus Florida
Early Fall

Cornus florida spp.
Fall Color

Cornus florida
F. Rubra

Cornus florida
Interesting Bark

Cornus kousa
Korean Dogwood

Description - A native to Korea, the Korean dogwood is rapidly becoming the dogwood of choice since it is not prone to lower dieback disease. Korean Dogwood is very similar to flowering dogwood in overall size, growth form and flower shape. Korean Dogwoods are known for the open and horizontal branching effect of its limbs as well as its four- season beauty. Great spring flowers, lovely summer foliage, rich fall color and fruit appearing later on in the fall. Korean dogwood grows slowly to manageable height and spread. The flowers are mostly white although recently, a pink variety has been introduced. Kousa flowers are slightly larger than those of the flowering dogwood. It is interesting to note that kousa dogwoods will flower up to a month later than the flowering dogwood. This also enhances its value as the bloom time arrives when not many other shrubs or trees are in bloom. A kousa dogwood in full bloom can be spectacular, a mountain of white!

Foliage is an attractive medium green color with slightly pointed leaves. In fall, the foliage turns to a burnt orange or burgundy color that is extremely good-looking. Prior to fall, Korean dogwood produces reddish-colored berries that contrast nicely against the foliage. The berries will last through the winter and attracts birds. Korean dogwoods are perfect for a specimen lawn tree or as a foundation plant to soften a corner.

Zones - 6 to 9

Height - 15 to 18 feet

Spread - up to 15 feet

Exposure - full sun to very light shade

Soil - Cornus kousa grows best in a well-drained soil that is rich in organic matter and slightly acidic.

Bloom time - May

Care - Cornus kousa can be difficult to grow if planted in the wrong location; give it full sun and a slightly acidic soil, and it will do fine. It is rarely bothered by insects or disease. Water moderately and do not water late in the day.

Cornus kousa spp.

Cornus kousa spp.

Cornus kousa spp.
Fall Color

Cornus kousa spp.
Late Summer

Cornus kousa spp.
Late Fall

Crataegus laevigata
English Hawthorne

Description - There are over one thousand species of hawthorne. The most commonly grown hawthorne is the English hawthorne. Noted for its pink flowers in spring and clusters of red berries in fall, English hawthorne is an excellent landscape tree. It has many outstanding features, but the single most important are the fall berries, which are more noticeable than the spring flowers. The berries are a vivid red color and grow in clusters, producing a great contrast against the deep green leaves. It is very handsome. The berries persist into winter and are a welcome source of food for songbirds. Flowers are, relatively small but abundant, appearing in early spring and putting on a nice display. The foliage, although nothing spectacular in summer, will turn an attractive rich bronze color in fall.

Crataegus laevigata spp.
Early Fall Berries

English hawthorne stays relatively small in size, growing to about 20 feet. It is ideal for a lawn specimen or mixed in the shrub border. Hawthorne can also be trained to create a hedge.

Zones - 4 to 9

Height - 16 to 22 feet

Spread - up to 15 feet

Exposure - full sun to light shade

Soil - Hawthorne grows best in a well-drained soil that is rich in organic matter.

Bloom time - late spring

Care - Hawthorne is moderately easy to grow. It can be susceptible to leaf blight and cedar apple rust, but spraying can remedy these problems. Water moderately and do not water late in the day.

Crataegus laevigata spp.
Fall color

Crataegus laevigata spp.

Crataegus laevigata spp.

Elaeagnus angustifolia
Russian Olive

Description - Russian olive is totally deer proof and is easy to grow. Having said that, I will tell you, it is not a tree with dramatic flowers or other great features. Perhaps the nicest single feature about Russian olive is that its foliage is very appealing. The foliage is narrow and reminds me of the weeping willow's foliage, with a beautiful silvery gray color. The sight and sound of Russian olive leaves shimmering in the breeze can be quite relaxing; it reminds one of Italy and Greece. Like all trees, Russian olive will flower; however, the flowers are quite small and inconspicuous.

Another interesting feature is Russian olive's bark, which has a gnarled and twisted look that is eye-catching. The best use for Russian olive is a windbreak or a seasonal screen. It also makes a very nice hedge as it readily accepts pruning or shearing.

Zones - 7 to 9

Height - 20 to 24 feet

Spread - up to 22 feet

Exposure - full sun to light shade

Soil - Russian olive grows best in a well-drained sandy soil, but it will grow anywhere.

Bloom time - April

Care - Russian olive is very easy to grow. No pest problems or disease problems plague this tree. Water moderately and do not water late in the day.

Elaeagnus angustifolia
Interesting Bark

Elaeagnus angustifolia

Enkianthus campanulatus
Redvein Enkianthus

Description - This small group of shrubs, native to
Japan, is not used enough in the home landscape.
Redvein is valued for their unusual flowers, which
are bell shaped much like lily of the valley. They
are white with red veins, giving them a pinkish cast.
The flowering display is not spectacular from a
distance but attractive when seen up close. Redvein
is especially prized and noted for its colorful display
of fall foliage. Yellow, orange, and red leaves are
available among species. All foliage choices are
brilliantly colored in fall and stand out at a distance.
The foliage in spring is also good-looking with
a sword-shaped leaf and a medium green color.
Redvein mixes very well with andromeda, mountain
laurel, and leucothoe as it also likes slightly acidic

Enkianthus campanulatus
Fall foliage

soil. It makes a nice foundation plant; it is a slow grower and will spread to only 8 feet over twenty years.
Another good use is a grouping of shrubs in an informal bed. While not a well-known plant, redvein should
definitely be considered in the deer-proof garden

Zones - 6 to 9

Height - 8 to 9 feet

Spread - up to 7 feet

Exposure - full sun to light shade

Soil - Redvein grows best in a well-drained soil that is rich in organic
matter and slightly acidic.

Bloom time - late spring

Care - Redvein is easy to grow. It has no major pest or disease
problems. Water moderately and do not water late in the day.

Enkianthus Campanulatus

Enkianthus campanulatus
Fall Color

Enkianthus campanulatus

Euonymus alatus
Burning Bush

Description - Let me say right off, all of the *Euonymus* species, except burning bush are a favorite food for deer. Burning bush is the one exception to the rule. Deer generally avoid burning bush throughout the year as it is poisonous. Burning bush is a large growing shrub eventually reaching a height of 15 feet with a spread of 15 feet! There are several smaller-growing cultivars available with compacta being the standard for the smaller growing species. Compacta will reach a height and spread of 8 feet. Burning bush is not a shrub with many redeeming features. The one outstanding feature burning bush offers is its brilliant fall foliage. If burning bush is positioned in full sun, the leaves in fall will turn to a flaming red color, hence the name burning bush. If planted in semishade, the leaf colors will not be nearly as red; instead, they become dark pink, almost the color of a rose wine. It is still attractive but not as noticeable as the red-color foliage. When using burning bush, be sure

Euonymus alatus
Fall foliage

to plant it in full sun. Burning bush does produce flowers in late spring, but they are insignificant and hardly worth mentioning. In spring and summer, the foliage is a medium to dark green color with leaves growing up to 3 inches long in a narrow shape; there is nothing unusual or exciting about them. Burning bush branches and stems do have an unusual shape, however. It is almost a cross shape and interesting to look at. It is important to note that burning bush can be invasive. In fact, I was surprised to learn that burning bush is prohibited in the state of Massachusetts due to its aggressive growth! Give it room to spread out, never planting it near the home foundation, as it will quickly outgrow the area. It does accept shearing, but that will destroy its natural growing shape, which is vase shaped in youth, changing to spreading and rounded as it ages. The best use for burning bush is a group planting toward the property edge, perhaps as a property boundary marker. Be sure to position where it is visible from a distance to observe the fall colors.

Zones - 4 to 8

Height - 8 to 15 feet (depending on species)

Spread - up to 15 feet

Exposure - full sun to light shade

Soil - Burning bush grows best in a well-drained soil that is rich in organic matter and slightly acidic.

Bloom time - late spring

Euonymus alatus
Compacta

Euonymus alatus
Interesting Branch Shape

Care - Burning bush is moderately easy to grow. It is sometimes troubled by winged euonymus scale, which can be remedied by spraying. Hardwood mulch can cause a nitrogen deficiency; this can be corrected by switching to a different type of mulch (pine needles work best) and fertilizing on an annual basis. Summer drought will cause problems; be sure to water thoroughly in summer and do not water late in the day.

Fagus
European Beech

Description – The European beech is a spectacular landscape tree that needs a lot of room to spread. I say this because it will eventually spread to 80 feet and reach a height of 50 to 80 feet. It should never be planted near a home as it will take over its environment. It needs to be positioned in an open area with plenty of room to spread as a large growing specimen should be.

Having said this, if you have such an area available for planting, European beech is unparalleled as a large landscape plant. A major reason is the foliage. The leaves are an appealing bright green in spring, oval and slightly pointed. In the fall, they turn a bronze to orange color. Some varieties such as atropunicea purpurea are purple leafed in spring and summer and turn a deeper purple/green in fall. Tricolor is truly spectacular as the leaves are deep green with a pink border all season, creating a spectacular contrast. In fall, the colors simply deepen to rich hues of red. Another strong point of European beech is its bark, which is a beautiful gray color. The overall growth habit of European beech is rounded with upright and spreading branches. There are also weeping and contorted varieties available, which will grow smaller than species. All in all, beech is a great plant for large open areas.

Zones - 5 to 9

Height - 50 to 80 feet

Spread - up to 80 feet

Exposure - full sun to light shade

Soil - Fagus grows best in a well-drained soil. It has no special soil requirements.

Care - Fagus is easy to grow. Plant it in a location where it can spread up to 80 feet.

Fagus
Tricolor

Fagus
Atropunicea purpurea

Fagus
Atropunicea purpurea

Fagus
Atropunicea purpurea

Fagus
Atropunicea grandifolia Fall Color

Forsythia
Forsythia

Description - Can there be any plant more easily recognized than forsythia in full bloom? Brilliant yellow blooms announcing spring, forsythia is one of the earliest bloomers. This is a plant that is truly grown for its flowers. When out of flower, forsythia is quite common looking and does little to distinguish itself.

However, the flowers more than make up for the lack of beauty during the rest of the growing season. The flowers are small but appear in such abundance that the whole plant appears covered in

Forsythia
Lynwood Gold

dainty yellow flowers. In fact, each flower appears on bare wood before the foliage appears, making the flowers stand out. The natural growth habit of forsythia is fountain shaped, spreading and drooping as a fountain would. All too often, it is pruned to become a hedge, and this destroys its natural shape. Forsythia will not bloom well unless winter temperatures are well below the freezing point.

Some of the best varieties of forsythia are linwood gold, which has very bright yellow flowers.

Spring glory has more toned down lemon yellow–colored flowers.

A recent cultivar, golden times has variegated green and yellow foliage making it highly unusual and attractive during the growing season. It is not easy to find however.

Forsythia's best use is as a lawn highlight or perhaps as an informal screen along property lines. It is also an excellent cut flower. Forsythia must be planted in full sun for the best flowers. It will grow in shade; however, it will not flower well.

Zones - 5 to 9

Height - 6 to 8 feet

Spread - up to 8 feet

Exposure - full sun

Soil - Forsythia grows best in a well-drained sandy, soil but it will grow anywhere.

Bloom time - early spring

Forsythia
Lynwood Gold

Care - Forsythia is very easy to grow. No pest problems or disease-related problems are prevalent with this plant. Water moderately and do not water late in the day.

Gleditsia traicanthos inermis
Honey Locust

Description - Honey locust makes for a fine lawn-specimen tree. With the dappled shade it creates, a lawn can grow right up to its trunk. Although it's not noted for its flowers, it does have small white blossoms that are similar to Wisteria flowers. They bloom in summer and are moderatly attractive. It should be noted that following the flowers, leathery seedpods appear. They are long, not attractive, and contain beanlike seeds. Finally, they create somewhat of a mess as far as litter is concerned. For this reason, it is unwise to plant honey locust near a deck or driveway. The leaves are finely cut and create a nice texture; in fall, they turn a brilliant yellow color, putting on quite a display. The honey locust's growth habit is upright and slightly open, allowing light below. It is a fairly quick grower, so give it room to grow. I find its best use is as a lawn-specimen tree, but keep in mind this is a large growing tree and requires room to spread; do not plant it close to the home. A nice cultivar is skyline, which has bright orange foliage in fall.

Zones - 3 to 10

Height - 25 to 70 feet

Spread - up to 50 feet

Exposure - full sun

Soil - Honey locust grows best in a well-drained soil, but it will grow almost anywhere.

Bloom time - May

Care - Honey locust is very easy to grow. Water moderately and do not water late in the day.

Gleditsia traicanthos inermis
Skyline

Gleditsia traicanthos inermis
Skyline
Fall color

Kolkwitzia amabilis
Beauty Bush

Description – Beauty bush is an old-fashioned shrub commonly used in the Victorian era. Many owners of historic homes are surprised to find that beauty bush played a large part in their original foundation plantings. It is indeed an aptly named shrub; I find it beautiful when in flower. Beauty bush's natural growing habit is vase shaped with weeping or arching stems. In spring, the entire plant is covered with trumpet-shaped pink flowers with yellow throats. Each flower is 2 to 3 inches across with five petals and very striking. There are a few cultivars available with white flowers and yellow throats, but the most widely used are the pink-flowering varieties. After flowering, slightly fuzzy berries appear that are also attractive. The foliage is oval shaped about 2 to 3 inches long but nothing spectacular to look at. Beauty bush should be planted in full sun for flowers. It will grow in shade; however, it will not flower of any consequence in shade. Some of the very best varieties of beauty bush are pink cloud and rosea. The best uses for beauty bush are as foundation plants or in a mixed shrub bed or as a lawn-specimen plant.

Kolkwitzia amabilis
Pink Cloud

Zones - 4 to 9

Height - 10 feet

Spread - up to 8 feet

Exposure - full sun

Soil - Beauty bush grows best in a well-drained sandy soil, but it tolerates most soil conditions.

Bloom time - May

Care - Beauty bush is very easy to grow. It has no serious pest or disease problems. Water moderately and do not water late in the day.

Kolkwitzia amabilis spp.

Oxydendrum arboreum
Sourwood

Description - Sourwood is a favored tree in my home landscape. I positioned it near the kitchen table window years ago, where we can enjoy the four-seasoned glory each day. Sourwood is a native tree that grows slowly to a neat upright position. I find it attractive all year because of its unusual features. The flowers are very similar to the bell shape of the lily of the valley in appearance and hang from racemes in midsummer. Although the flowers are small in size, they bloom abundantly. The foliage is lance shaped and an attractive dark green color in season. In early fall, sourwood foliage turns a brilliant scarlet red. At the same time, pearl color seedpods have formed, and the contrast of seedpods hanging in racemes against the red foliage is beautiful and unusual! Sourwood is one of the earliest trees to turn to its fall colors, bringing a new season into focus. In winter, I enjoy the form of the tree against the skyline without foliage. It seems older and more gnarled than it should be by its years. The bark is also interesting in that it is coarse and bold. As an added bonus, the seedpods persist into winter, adding more drama to the winter skyline. If it sounds like I love this plant, it is true: it *is* a great plant. Be sure to plant sourwood near a major window, patio, or deck—where it can be observed yearlong. Some of the best uses for sourwood is either as a lawn-specimen tree or in the foundation bed to soften a corner.

Zones - 3 to 9

Height - 35 feet

Spread - up to 20 feet

Exposure - partial shade

Soil - Sourwood grows best in a well-drained acidic soil.

Bloom time - May

Care - Sourwood is very easy to grow. No disease or pests plague this plant. Water moderately and do not water late in the day.

***Oxydendrum arboreum* spp.**
Fall Color

Oxydendrum arboreum
Spring

Oxydendrum arboreum

Oxydendrum arboreum
Summer

Oxydendrum arboreum
Interesting Bark

Prunus serrulata
Japanese Flowering Cherry

Description - Let me say right off, 99.9 percent of cherry species (prunus) are considered gourmet food by deer. Of all the prunus species, and there are many, Japanese flowering cherry is the most deer resistant. The other species will be heavily browsed by deer. Deer will not feed heavily on Japanese flowering cherry (*Prunus serrulata*). I have had several plants on my property for years with very little, if any, browsing on each tree. If you are looking for a showy flowering tree with attractive bark as a bonus, I recommend Japanese flowering cherry.

Prunus serrulta
Kwanzan

To start, the flowers of Japanese cherry are truly spectacular. Most cultivars have pink flowers, but there are a few choices with white flowers. The flowers are small and delicate but bloom in such profusion that the entire tree appears covered in blossoms in midspring. The foliage is also very appealing. In spring, each leaf is a finely shaped medium green color. In fall, they will turn various shades of bronze to a deep red color. The bark is beautiful with a rich cherry color that is distinctive only in cherries. It is very smooth to the touch and has a slight luster to it.

The normal growth form for Japanese cherry is vase shaped and upright. There is also a weeping Japanese cherry variety. Generally speaking, it is a small-size tree growing only 18 feet. Japanese cherries always seem to look in place. One of the best cultivar is kwanzan, which grows in a vase form to about 15 feet. Kwanzan is more deer resistant than its relatives; the growth being vase shaped helps keep the foliage on a six-foot tree stay out of reach of browsing deer.

Japanese cherries make excellent lawn highlight specimens trees or foundation plants to soften and hide corners or as a centerpiece in an informal bed.

Zones - 6 to 9

Height -18 feet

Spread - up to 15 feet

Exposure - full sun to light shade

Soil - Kwanzan grows best in a well-drained soil.

Bloom time - April/May

Care - Kwanzan is moderately easy to grow. A few insect species will go after this tree. Look for Japanese beetle to be prevalent. Spraying will remedy most of the insect-related problems. Water moderately and do not water late in the day.

Prunus serrulta
Kwanzan

Prunus serrulta Kwanzan
Beautiful Bark Color and Texture

Prunus serrulta Kwanzan
Fall Color

Prunus serrulta
Kwanzan

Salix matsudana tortuosa
Corkscrew Willow

Description - Corkscrew willow is not a commonly used plant; however, it is unusual in its growth form and will attract attention. The single most important feature of corkscrew willow is its growth form. It grows in a highly unusual pattern of twisting and contorting its limbs. It is especially dramatic in winter when it has no foliage as its form will be truly appreciated and highlighted against the snow or the winter sky. Many florist use corkscrew willow foliage and stems in their arrangements to add drama to the arrangement.

The foliage in spring and summer are narrow-shaped bright green leaves that are delicate in appearance. The flowers are very inconspicuous and hardly worth mentioning.

Use corkscrew willow as a plant to create winter interest but not as a feature plant. It is not a good landscape tree for many situations due to its invasive root system, limb dieback, and short life span. I feel the best uses for corkscrew willow are in an informal bed mixed with other interesting plants that will compliment its unusual growth form. The best use may be in boggy/wet areas as a filler plant as it performs well in this situation. I like evergreen ground covers beneath corkscrew willow to add a base to its unusual form.

Zones - 5 to 10

Height - 35 feet

Spread - up to 30 feet

Exposure - full sun

Soil - Willow grows best in a well-drained soil, but it will grow anywhere. It will also perform well in wet, boggy areas.

Care - Willow are very easy to grow. Water moderately and do not water late in the day.

Salix matsudana tortuosa spp.

Sassafras albidum
Common Sassafras

Description - Sassafras is another plant
not well known or widely used by
professionals in the garden landscape.
I am not sure why, sassafras adds value
to the landscape. Sassafras can be truly
spectacular in fall with blazing color. It
has some unusual characteristics that
make it both interesting and unique.
For example, sassafras leaves have three
distinct shapes, all appearing on the
same tree. Some leaves are smooth
and oval, others are smooth on one
side and indented on the other (like a
mitten), and the rest can be indented
on both sides. The foliage during the
spring and summer are delicate and
finely cut with bright green leaves.
Sassafras does have early spring flowers
that appear before the leaves. They
are light yellow and attractive but not
very showy. I would say the single most
important feature of sassafras is the fall foliage colors, which
can range from orange to red or purple.

Sassafras albidum
Early Fall Color

One of the best uses for sassafras is as a hedgerow. This is due
to its natural growing habit, which is spreading. Sassafras will
grow in thickets and spread establishing itself quickly. Another
good use for sassafras is as a mass planting at the woodland
edge. This will highlight from a distance the spectacular fall
color that is sure to come.

Zones - 6 to 9

Height - 30 feet

Spread - up to 30 feet

Exposure - full sun

Soil - Sassafras grows best in a well-drained, rich soil slightly
acidic such as a natural woodland.

Care - Sassafras is very easy to grow. Water moderately and do
not water late in the day.
Remove suckers if single-stem plants are desired.

Sassafras albidum

Sassafras albidum
Late Fall color

Spiraea vanhouttei and Spiraea prunifolia
Spiraea

Description - Spiraea is a shrub that while often
used in landscapes is known primarily for its
flowers. When out of bloom, it is quite ordinary
and not noticeable. No other quality of spiraea
distinguishes itself beyond the flowers. There
are many different varieties of spiraea available
from dwarf-size, to large-size, to robust-size
shrubs. The most popular cultivars are bridal
wreath (prunifolia) and vanhoutte. Incidentally,
from a deer-resistance standpoint, the only
cultivars of spiraea I would recommend is bridal
wreath and vanhoutte; the other cultivars
are browsed by deer much more frequently.
These two shrubs both have clusters of white
flowers in spring and grow quite large. Some
varieties come with pink flowers, but the most
commonly used spiraea is the white flower
choices. The flowers itself are small, but they
all bloom together and put on a nice display
lasting about two weeks. Some cultivars like the
above two flower in May while others flower
in June. The basic form of spiraea is arching
or fountainlike in its youth. As it gets older,
it grows more leggy and open, sometimes
becoming twiggy. I recommend planting spiraea
as a specimen plant in an area where it can
spread. Since it is quite a large shrub, it requires
open space. Another common use is as an
informal hedge.

Zones - 5 to 10

Height - 10 to 12 feet

Spread - up to 12 feet

Exposure - full sun

Soil - Spiraea grows best in a normal well
-drained garden soil—not too rich or acidic.

Bloom time - May–June

Spiraea Vanhoutte

Spiraea vanhoutte

Care - Spiraea are fairly easy to grow. They can
be susceptible to powdery mildew disease, which can be treated by spraying. There are a number of insects that
feed upon this plant. A regular treatment of pesticide will alleviate this problem. Woody older plants should be
cut back to the ground in early spring, to rejuvenate.

Syringa vulgaris
Common Lilac

Description - Lilac is an old-time shrub, very commonly used in the Victorian era. It seems quite at home in the border of a Victorian- or a Tudor-style home. Lilacs are especially prized for their highly fragrant flowers. The most popular species is the lavender-color flower species; however, there are literally hundreds of species available with bloom colors ranging from white, to pink, to purple, or to blue. Some of the best are alba (white), President Lincoln (lavender), and Charles Jolly (purple). Although I find the foliage to be relatively attractive with their heart-shaped leaves, lilacs are grown primarily for their flowers. The flowers are quite small but bloom in great profusion at the top of stemming branches. A lilac in full bloom is an impressive sight. The basic growth form of lilac is vase shaped and spreading. They form thickets in growth, which are multi stemming and will spread over time. Lilac must be positioned in full sun for the best flowering results. If planted in shade, the flowering will be poor, and the plant will be subject to powdery mildew disease, which will be severe. I strongly recommend planting lilac near a deck, near a patio, or near a screen door to take advantage of its delightfully scented flowers. Another great use is as a hedge along the walkway. Lilacs are also an excellent choice for a cut-flower bed.

Syringa vulgaris
President Lincoln

Zones - 5 to 9

Height - 5 to 18 feet

Spread - up to 18 feet

Exposure - full sun

Soil - Lilacs grow best in a well-drained, rich soil that is slightly acidic.

Bloom time - May–June

Care - Lilacs are easy to grow. Remove suckers if a single-stem plant is desired. Lilac can be susceptible to powdery mildew disease, which can be treated by spraying. Woody older plants need to be cut back to the ground to rejuvenate.

Syringa vulgaris
Alba and Charles Jolly

Syringa vulgaris spp.

Syringa vulgaris

Plant List for Quick Reference

The below list should be used as a reference for situating plants in problem areas and/or as an outstanding feature reference.

The first section highlights such problems as shady spots, sandy soil, heavy clay soil, etc. These problem areas require plants that are able to perform in this environment, where other species cannot.

The second section details the plants with outstanding features during the growing seasons. Showy berries in fall, outstanding flowers, attractive fall foliage—the type of features that make a plant standout.

Section 1

Deer-Proof Annuals for Shade
Begonia × Semperflorens cultorum
- Wax Begonia
Myosotis sylvatica - Forget-Me-Not
Salvia splendens - Salvia

Deer-Proof Perennials for Shade
Anemone species - Anemone
Aquilegia species - Columbine
Aruncus dioicus - Goatsbeard
Astible - Meadowsweet
Bergenia - Bergenia
Campanula - Bellflower
Cimicifuga racemosa - Bugbane
Dicentra species - Bleeding Heart
Echinacea purpurea - Purple Coneflower
Filipendula - Queen of the Prairie
Helleborus niger - Hellebore
Monarda – Bee Balm
Osmunda cinnamomea - Cinnamon Fern
Osmunda regalis - Royal Fern
Polystichum species - Fern
Primula species - Primrose
Pulmonaria saccharata - Lungwort

Deer-Proof Ground Covers for Shade
Ajuga reptans - Bugleweed
Convallaria majalis - Lily of the Valley
Epimedium species - Barrenwort
Pachysandra terminallis
- Japanese Pachysandra
Vinca minor - Periwinkle

Deer-Proof Vines for Semishade
Clematis species - Clematis
Wisteria species - Wisteria

Deer-Proof Shrubs and Trees for Shade
Buxus - Boxwood (semishade)
Cornus florida - Flowering Dogwood
Cornus kousa - Kousa Dogwood (semishade)
Enkianthus - Red Vein Enkianthus
Ilex opaca - American Holly
Ilex cornuta - Chinese Holly
Kalmia latifolia - Mountain Laurel
Leucothoe fontanesia - Drooping Leucothoe
Oxydendrum aboreum - Sourwood
Pieris japonia - Japanese Pieris

Deer-Proof Slope Stabilizers
Cotoneaster - Cotoneaster
Lonicera - Honeysuckle
Vinca - Periwinkle
Epimedium - Barrenwort

Deer-Proof Lawn Alternatives (for large areas)
Ajuga - Bugleweed
Pachysandra terminalis - Japanese Spurge
Vinca - Periwinkle

Deer-Proof Trees and Shrubs for Sandy Soils
Betula Pendula - European White Birch
Kolkwitzia - Beauty Bush
Yucca - Yucca

Deer-Proof Perennials for Sandy Soil
Achillea - Yarrow
Artemsia - Wormwood
Dianthus - Sweet William, Pinks
Echinops - Globe Thistle
Gypsophila - Baby's Breath

Deer-Proof Annuals for Sandy Soils
Coreopsis (some) - Coreopsis
Lobularia - Sweet Alyssum
Papaver - Poppy
Tagetes - Marigold
Verbena - Verbena

Deer-Proof Trees and Shrubs for Clay Soils
Oxydendrum arboreum - Sourwood
Kalmia latifolia - Mountain Laurel

Deer-Proof Perennials for Clay Soils
Aruncus dioicus - Goatsbeard
Filipendula ulmaria - Queen of the Prairie
Lythrum - Loosestrife

Deer-Proof Trees and Shrubs for Chalk and Limestone Soils
Berberis - Barberry
Pinus Nigra - Austrian Pine
Syringa - Lilac
Yucca - Yucca

Deer-Proof Climbers for Chalk and Limestone Soil
Clematis - Clematis
Lonicera - Honeysuckle
Wisteria - Wisteria

Deer-Proof Annuals and Perennials for Chalk and Limestone Soil
Achillea - Yarrow
Ageratum - Ageratum
Alyssum - Basket of Gold
Bergenia - Bergenia
Campanula - Bellflower
Dianthus - Pinks
Lobularia martitima - Sweet Alyssum
Papaver - Poppy
Salvia - Salvia
Tagetes - Marigold
Veronica - Speedwell

Deer-Proof Trees and Shrubs for Acidic Soil
Cotoneaster species - Cotoneaster
Ilex species(most) - Holly
Kalmia latifolia - Mountain Laurel
Leucothoe species - Leucothoe
Picea species - Spruce
Pieris species - Andromeda
Pinus species (most) - Pine

Section 2

Deer-Proof Trees with Showy Berries or Fruits
Cornus florida - Flowering Dogwood
Cornus kousa - Kousa Dogwood
Crataegus phaenopyrum
- Washington Hawthorne
Oxydendrum aboreum - Sourwood

Deer-Proof Shrubs with Showy Berries or Fruit
Berberis darwinii - Darwin Barberry
Berberis koreana - Korean Barberry
Berberis thunbergii - Japanese Barberry
Cotoneaster dammeri
- Bearberry Cotoneaster
Cotoneaster divaricata
- Spreading Cotoneaster
Cotoneaster horizontalis
- Rock-spray Cotoneaster
Ilex cornuta - Chinese Holly
Ilex opaca - American Holly
Pinus strobus - White Pine

Deer-Proof Trees with Showy Bark
Betula papyrifera - Paper Birch
Betula pendula - European White Birch
Cornus florida - Flowering Dogwood
Cornus kousa - Kousa Dogwood
Elaeagnus augustifolia - Russian Olive
Oxydendrum arboreum - Sourwood
Pinus nigra - Austrian Pine
Prunus serrulata - Japanese Flowering Cherry

Deer-Proof Trees with Interesting Summer Foliage
Cornus florida - Flowering Dogwood
Cornus kousa - Kousa Dogwood
Fagus sylvatica (Purpurea, Riversi, Rohanni, tricolor)
- European Beech
Oxydendrum arboreum - Sourwood
Picea pungens - Colorado Blue Spruce

Deer-Proof Trees and Shrubs with Brilliant Fall Foliage
Betula papyrifera - Paper Birch
Betula pendula - European White Birch
Cotoneaster - Cotoneaster
Cornus florida - Flowering Dogwood
Cornus kousa - Kousa Dogwood
Crataegus - English Hawthorne
Enkianthus campanulatus
- Redvein Enkianthus
Euonymus alatus - Burning Bush
Fagus sylvatica - European Beech
Leucothoe fontamesiana - Leucothoe
Oxydendrum arboreum - Sourwood
Prunus serrulata - Flowering Cherry

Deer-Proof Trees and Shrubs with Outstanding Flowers
Cornus florida - Flowering Dogwood
Cornus kousa - Kousa Dogwood
Crataegus laevigata - English Hawthorne
Enkianthus campanulatus
- Redvein Enkianthus
Forsythia - Forsythia
Kolkwitzia - Beauty Bush
Leucothoe fontamesiana - Leucothoe
Oxydendrum arboreum - Sourwood
Pieris - Andromeda
Prunus serrulata - Flowering Cherry
Spiraea - Spiraea
Syringa vulgaris - Common Lilac

Plants to Avoid Using in the Deer-Proof Garden

The plants below are the absolute favorite foods for deer. I strongly suggest not using these plants in your landscape as they are sure to be devoured by deer. Some species will be browsed in the middle of spring when deer normally feed away from our homes as deer simply find these plants irresistible.

Unfortunately, there are very attractive plants on this list, commonly used in areas without deer problems. Species like rhododendron and euonymus are beautiful, but they will only cause you frustration if you use them. I have found that although you can never replace a rhododendron, for example, you can use other species that have attractive flowers and that bloom the same time as rhododendron and have the same effect.

Annuals
Alcea Rosea - Hollyhocks
Impatiens - Impatiens
Tithonia rotundifolia - Mexican Sunflower

Perennials
Crocus
Hemerocallis species - Daylily (most)
Hosta species - Hosta
Lobella cardinalis - Cardinal Flower
Phlox - Phlox
Rosa species - Rose
Tulipa species - Tulips

Shrubs and Trees
Abies balsamea - Balsam Fir
Abies fraseri - Fraser Fir
Acer platanoides - Norway Maple
Cercis canadensis - Eastern Redbud
Chamaecyparis thyoides - Atlantic White Cedar
Cornus mas - Cornelian Dogwood
Euonymus - most species (except Alatus)
Hedera helix - English Ivy
Malus species - Apples
Prunus species (most) - Cherries
Prunus species - Plums
Rhododendron species - Rhododendron
Rhododendron species - Azaleas
Rosa × hybrid - Hybrid Tea Rose
Sorbus aucuparia - European Mountain Ash
Taxus species - Yews
Thuja species - Arborvitae

I hope you have enjoyed reading my deer-proof planting
book as much as I have enjoyed writing it.

Please feel free to visit me at our Web site,
www.creatingadeerproofgarden.com
should you have any further deer-related landscape
problems or questions. In the future, we will be offering
deer-proof plantings, our own proprietary line of
deer-repellent spray, and a selection of the best
gardening gloves and tools

Peter Derano